Vocational education and training in the developed world

Vocational education and training in the developed world
A comparative study

Leonard Cantor

R

ROUTLEDGE
London and New York

First published 1989
by Routledge
11 New Fetter Lane, London EC4P 4EE
29 West 35th Street, New York NY 10001

© 1989 Leonard Cantor

Phototypeset in 10pt Times by
Mews Photosetting, Beckenham, Kent
Printed and bound in Great Britain by
Biddles Ltd, Guildford and King's Lynn

British Library Cataloguing in Publication Data

Cantor, Leonard M. (Leonard Martin), *1927–*
    Vocational education and training in the
    developed world: a comparative study.
    1. Developed countries. Vocational
    education. Vocational training. Vocational
    education & training
    I. Title
    370.11'3'091722

    ISBN 0-415-02541-9
    ISBN 0-415-02542-7 Pbk

Library of Congress Cataloging-in-Publication Data

Cantor, Leonard Martin.
    Vocational education and training in the developed world: a
    comparative study / Leonard Cantor.
        p. cm.
    Bibliography: p.
    Includes index.
    ISBN 0-415-02541-9. ISBN 0-415-02542-7 (pbk.)
    1. Vocational education — Cross-cultural studies. 2. Occupational
training — Cross-cultural studies. I. Title.
    LC1043.C36   1989
    370.11'3–dc19   88-29353
                                                                          CIP

Contents

List of Figures

List of Tables

Preface

The purpose of this book is, in broad terms, relatively simple and clear: to provide a series of pictures of the provision of vocational education and training in five countries in the developed world, including the United Kingdom and its principal industrial competitors — namely Japan, Australia, the United States, and the Federal Republic of Germany. It also aims to draw some comparisons between these countries and the United Kingdom which should be informative and thought-provoking for the British reader for whom this book is primarily intended. At the outset, it is apparent that the provision of vocational education and training throughout the countries being surveyed is subject to a rapid and increasingly exponential degree of change. The descriptions of the national systems which follow are, therefore, in the nature of 'snapshots' which identify their major characteristics as they were at the time of writing, namely at the end of 1987.

While the book's purpose may be relatively simple, its use of terminology is a much more complex matter, never more so than in the term embraced in its title, 'vocational education and training'. Much could be and, indeed, has been written on the subject, but any attempt to draw too fine distinctions between 'education' and 'training' or between 'vocational education' and 'vocational training', for example, would be unprofitable. For one thing, the terms are used differently in different countries, for another it would unnecessarily restrict the scope of this book, and for a third, in the words of King Lear, 'that way madness lies'. However, some indication of the way in which the terms are used is clearly necessary, if only because, as Twining points out,[1] the drawing of boundaries between them can, in many countries, influence who does what and who pays for what.

For the sake of relative simplicity, therefore, the term 'vocational education and training' is taken to connote those learning activities, including the acquisition of skills, which contribute to successful economic performance.[2] It thus excludes the provision of general education provided in school systems, though it does include the occupational-specific programmes offered by American high schools and the work-related 'Arbeitslehre' studies offered in West German schools. To distinguish further between 'vocational education' on the one hand and 'training' on the other, the former is taken to comprise job-related programmes offered by educational establishments, such as the American Community College, or the Japanese Special School, while the latter refers generally to job-specific programmes offered by industry. Even here, however, the distinction is not entirely clear cut, as training, offered by Japanese industry for example, is infused by a strong desire to attend to the moral and cultural education of their employees.

In order to keep the book within manageable proportions, the scope of vocational education and training so defined is restricted to the preparation of skilled personnel at what in British terms would be described as operative, craft and technician levels. For this reason, the British chapter, for example, concentrates on vocational courses provided in Non-Advanced Further Education (NAFE), that is, primarily technical colleges and colleges of further education, and excludes those at advanced level offered by Universities, Polytechnics and Colleges and Institutes of Higher Education. Similarly, in Australia, the work of the institutions of Technical and Further Education (TAFE) is examined in detail while that of the Universities and Colleges of Advanced Education is excluded. In practice, of course, there is inevitably a degree of overlap: for one thing, it is not always crystal clear what precisely constitutes non-advanced further education as distinct from advanced, and for another, many British and Australian technical colleges, for example, offer some advanced courses while their advanced counterparts, the Colleges of Higher Education provide, in varying degrees, non-advanced courses.

As systems of vocational education and training reflect in microcosm the societies of which they are part and can only be properly comprehended in their broader context, so in each of the chapters dealing with individual countries there is an introductory section briefly delineating the relevant social and educational background. Where relevant and appropriate, in the chapters describing national systems of vocational education certain major themes are described and analysed, including provision for unemployed young people, ethnic minorities, and women and girls; and the training of teachers and instructors of vocational subjects.

As will quickly become apparent from reading this book, systems of vocational education and training are extremely varied and diverse, catering as they do, not only for an enormous range of industrial and business activities, but also for a greater variety of students than any other sector of education. Thus, the latter range in age from those who are in school through those just leaving schools to experienced adults who are updating their skills or retraining for new jobs. Equally varied are the bases of study, from full-time and sandwich courses of varying lengths, to very large numbers of part-time courses, whether in colleges or the workplace, to an increasing provision of programmes based on 'distance learning' or external studies.

In conclusion, vocational education and training operates across a very broad spectrum from general education at one extreme to very narrow vocational training on the other. At best, however, it encompasses what Twining[3] calls 'a dual mandate', that is to say, it develops the individual both in his own interests and also to the benefit of his employment.

Acknowledgements

I have to thank very many people who, in a variety of ways, have helped me to bring this book to fruition. First, I am grateful to the Leverhulme Foundation for the award of a Research Fellowship which greatly facilitated the research which I undertook in Japan, Australia and the United States. Among those who were of considerable help to me in these three countries, a number deserve special mention. In Japan they include Hiroshi Kimura and Yoshihito Yasuhara of the National Institute for Educational Research, Tokyo; Toshio Ishikawa, Adviser to the Japanese Institute of Labour; Maurice Jenkins, Education Officer, British Council, Tokyo; Kisaku Miyasaka, Professor of Adult Education, University of Tokyo; Professor Hiroshi Tsunogae, Shizuoka University; and Professor Shiuchi Kobe, Jyotesu Kyoiku University. In Australia, Professors Peter Fensham and Peter Musgrave, School of Education, Monash University, Clayton, Victoria; Professor Grant Harman, Centre for Administrative and Higher Education Studies, University of New England, New South Wales; and Dr Norm Pyle, Department of Technical and Further Education, Brisbane, Queensland. In the United States, Tom Worcester of Clackamas, Oregon; Al Philpott, Miami, Florida; Dr David Tyack, School of Education, Stanford University, California; Dr Tim Wentling, Office of Vocational Education Research, University of Illinois at Urbana-Champaign; Dr David Stern, School of Education, University of California, Berkeley. A number of people read individual chapters or parts of chapters for me, including Yoshihito Yasuhara and Toshio Ishikawa on Japan; Ross Harrold of the Centre for Admininistrative and Higher Education Studies, University of New England, Dr Norm Pyle, Dr Peter West, Director, The Wester Sydney Project, Nepean College of Advanced Education, and Kathleen Mackie of the Department of Employment, Education and Training, on Australia; and my long-time friend and co-author, Iolo Roberts, on the United Kingdom. While they all made extremely valuable suggestions to improve the respective chapters and pointed out numerous errors which had crept in, the responsibility for what remains and the views expressed are entirely mine.

Finally, I wish to thank Marjorie Salsbury for the enormous amount of typing and retyping that was necessary before the typescript achieved its final form. Above all, I am grateful to my wife for so tolerantly and encouragingly endured the protracted labours associated with the writing of this book.

Leonard Cantor

Loughborough, March 1988

Chapter one

Japan: A well-ordered society

In an article on Japanese Vocational Education and Training written a few years ago,[1] I commented on the fact that, given the astonishing post-war success of Japan's economy and its effects on its principal competitors, including the United Kingdom, it has been inevitable that we should seek reasons for that success and, where appropriate, emulate them. There is a widespread belief that an important contributory factor has been the Japanese system of vocational education and training, and it is the purpose of this chapter to describe and analyse that system and to judge whether that belief is justified.

Until relatively recently, however, very little has been written on the subject in The United Kingdom, and it was as late as 1984 that interest in it was stimulated in both educational and industrial circles, by the Report of the Institute of Manpower Studies, *Competence and Competition*, which reviewed vocational education and training policies, not only in Japan, but also in the Federal Republic of Germany and the United States.[2] To its own satisfaction and to that of many others, the Report, which was commissioned by the Manpower Services Commission (MSC) and the National Economic Development Organisation (NEDO), demonstrated what it called 'the central importance of vocational education and training in the development, production and selling of high quality, competitive products and services'. Its findings generated widespread discussion, and, as a result, comparisons have been drawn between the inadequacy of the British system of vocational education and training, and the effective programmes of major industrial competitors, including Japan. Another Report,[3] published two years later by the Society of Education Officers, based on a short visit to Japan in February 1986, reinforced the findings and recommendations of its predecessor.

The social background

One of the major difficulties that the authors of these reports faced was in trying to understand properly the cultural and social context of the countries under examination, particularly in the case of Japan, whose values and attitudes are so different to those widely found in developed countries in the west and where language differences pose formidable barriers, especially as both reports were based on visits lasting little more than two weeks. Nor would I claim much greater understanding, even though I lived in Japan and extensively examined Japanese vocational education and training for a period of four months in the Autumn of 1985. There is, however, a growing volume of literature both on Japanese society in general, and on its educational system in particular, mainly by American scholars, and three very informative books which are particularly to be recommended to those who wish to inform themselves more fully on these subjects, are Christopher's *The Japanese Mind: the Goliath explained*, Duke's *The Japanese School*, and Rohlen's *Japan's High Schools*.[4]

What then are the major cultural and social features of contemporary Japanese society which determine and influence their system of vocational education and training, as identified by these and other authors and which, indeed, are there for any percipient visitor to Japan to see? In some ways, perhaps the most significant is the widespread recognition of the need to utilise to the full the talents and abilities of the Japanese people. Japan is a country three-quarters of which is mountainous and uninhabitable, so that its population of 120 million is crowded into about 80,000 square kilometres, one-quarter of its total land surface of 378,000 square kilometres, and less than half the total land area of the United Kingdom. Moreover, it possesses very few natural resources, so that in order to survive it has to import large quantities of major raw materials such as oil, coal, iron ore, cotton, and wool, as well as wheat and other foodstuffs. Indeed, its only major resource is the talent of its people, which, it is generally agreed, must be developed and used to the full. This attitude is fostered by the relative social homogeneity of its population and by deep-rooted historical factors.

Japan's ethnic and social homogeneity is one of the features that most strikes the visitors: there is a virtual uniformity of skin and hair colour, for example, which is a marked contrast to the multi-ethnic societies of the United States, Australia and the United Kingdom. Foreigners, known to the Japanese as *Gaijin* are few and far between, especially outside the large cities: when my wife and I, for example, visited a small, rural primary school on the west coast of the main island, Honshu, we were told by the headmistress that we were the first westerners the children had seen. More significantly, perhaps, the only ethnic and social minorities are relatively small groups of Koreans, Ainu (natives of the northern island of Hokkaido), and *Burakumin*, or outcasts. The Koreans, who number fewer than 100,000, have lived in Japan for many years, but have been made to acquire Japanese nationality and are discriminated against in a variety of ways. The Burakumin, who to all outward appearances are indistinguishable from the rest of Japanese society, used formerly to live in ghettos but are now scattered about the country. They, too, suffer discrimination in a variety of ways, and tend to be restricted to less sought-after and more menial jobs. Recently, however, both groups have reacted more strongly against the somewhat scornful attitude of Japanese society and are increasingly demanding to be treated on a par with Japanese at large.

In many paradoxical ways, Japanese society is both much more hierarchical and classless than those in the west. The sense of hierarchy is well-developed on a personal level, determined by such factors as age and position in a company or educational institution, and manifested openly, for example, by the subtle ways in which Japanese address each other and the depths of their bows. On the other hand, the Japanese frequently claim that theirs is a classless society in which educational and other opportunities are equally available to all. To an extent this is true, as we shall see in the case of the educational system, and what Christopher calls 'some of the more obvious benchmarks of social class' in the West are missing in Japan: workers and university professors are likely to speak with similar accents and read the same newspaper, for example. On the other hand, there are clearly notable differences in the behaviour and standard of living of different groups in Japanese society which are linked to economic, educational and occupational status.

Another striking and immediately apparent feature of Japanese society is that it is socially cohesive and, perhaps as a consequence, extremely well-behaved. Anti-social behaviour is rare and frowned upon and it is possible, for example, to walk in any large city in Japan, at any time of day or night, without fear of molestation. This may also be a reflection of the fact that Japan is a very crowded, urbanised society. The great majority of its people live in large, very densely packed cities in which space is a premium, living space is extremely limited and very expensive, and where good social behaviour is essential to public order. By western standards, the cities are largely unplanned and visually nondescript and sometimes ugly — they were virtually all destroyed during the war and have since been rebuilt in the modern architectural vernacular. They have also greatly expanded, attracting many people from the countryside into Japan's booming industry and business, and seemingly go on for ever. On the other hand, for those who live in Japan's cities, their seemingly unending sprawl is humanised by falling into relatively small districts, each with its market area composed of stalls and small shops — the density of the cities for the most part obviates against chains of large supermarkets in the western idiom — and, more often than not, its temple. Above all, for foreigners at least, living in a large city is made more than bearable by the friendliness, warm hospitality and grace of virtually all the Japanese whom they encounter. It is one of the many paradoxes of Japan that it has permitted its cities to become visually ugly while retaining its love of simplicity and beauty in its gardens and, frequently, its house interiors.

Another reason for its relative social tranquility is the prevailing attitude, common also in China from which Japan has inherited much of its culture, which regards membership of a group as all-important, in sharp contradistinction to the much more individualistic attitudes adopted in the west. Indeed, membership of a group is seen as enhancing the importance of the individual so that there is little or no feeling of resentment at the loss of individual identity. In any case, as we have seen, individual identity and one's place in the scheme of things can be expressed in many subtle ways. It was pointed out to me by an American who was married to a Japanese wife, and who taught in one of the most prestigious Japanese universities, that the more reticent attitudes of the British were much more acceptable to the Japanese than the outgoing behaviour of the majority of Americans. The importance attached to being a member of a group was also brought home in another way: on visiting one of the technical colleges run by the Hitachi corporation for its employees, I was observing part of the training of a group of young graduates, recently recruited in strict competition from all over the country, who had embarked on a fifteen-month residential course, living in purpose-built accommodation. I was informed that, during the fifteen months, they were entitled to ten days holiday to return to their families if they wished, but many of them did not take it all up, preferring to spend their leisure time with their colleagues. This attitude, which admittedly is showing some signs of changing in the younger generation, breeds loyalty to companies and greatly reduces the likelihood of industrial dissent.

Along with the loyalty displayed by workers towards their companies, one frequently finds paternalistic attitudes adopted by many large companies towards their employees. This accounts for the strong tradition of 'life-long employment' which, to a limited extent, still prevails in certain grades in all large organisations, and for a wide range of company-provided fringe benefits. These attitudes, together with the national importance attached to developing the abilities of Japan's human resources, combine to lead Japanese companies to invest very heavily in industrial training and retraining. Indeed, of the total expenditure on industrial training in Japan, approximately three-quarters is provided by industry itself, and only one-quarter by the public sector.[5]

However, Japanese industry and business have been under increasing strain during the past few years. The combination of the rapid rise in the value of the yen, to which the term *endaka* is applied, has resulted in labour costs in Japan greatly exceeding those in countries like Korea, Taiwan and Singapore which are emerging as industrial rivals. One consequence has been a slow but steady rise in unemployment, which officially was running at just over 3 per cent in mid-1987. However, this figure conceals the fact that if the British method of calculating the rate of unemployment were used in Japan it would be at least twice as high there, as anyone who works for even a short period in the week is considered to be employed. Characteristically, the Japanese have responded to this situation with vigour. On the one hand, they are endeavouring to reduce labour costs by extending the use of automation and information technology. On the other, in keeping with the country's group psychology, Japanese industry is very reluctant to lay off their workers and instead, with government financial and other assistance, resort to measures such as transferring redundant workers to other companies, giving them longer holidays, and helping them to obtain other jobs.

It is worth commenting upon the fact that the skilled worker in Japan is expected not just to develop expertise in one skill to the exclusion of all others, but to be both adaptable and flexible in his attitude and skills in order to contribute more fully to the prosperity of his company. For this reason, Japanese industry provides both initial and retraining programmes. This combination of 'in house' education and training and social attitudes among employees, which has deep historical roots, results in a homogeneous corporate climate which often reaches religious or spiritual intensity.

There is a widespread acceptance in Japan, both by industry and the community at large, of the need for state facilitation of vocational training and, indeed, of a high degree of centralised control of the educational system. Thus, there is a long tradition of government involvement, both in establishing national economic goals, and in setting up and overseeing a framework of industrial training and development. The national statutory framework and administrative structure for industrial training are complex and based primarily upon the Vocational Training Law of 1969 and its subsequent amendments which lay down the fundamental principles of vocational training and make provision for the roles to be played by the various parties concerned with these activities.

Perhaps the major feature of this framework is that the primary responsibility for providing vocational training rests with industry, and the state, through the Ministry of Labour, assists in this process in a variety of ways, by, for example, providing substantial subsidies to encourage smaller companies to provide the necessary training. The government also oversees a national system of trade testing which has been in existence since 1959. It now extends to no fewer than 102 trades and operates at two levels, Grade I (more advanced) and Grade II. The tests are provided once a year and are a considerable stimulus to workers to undergo additional training, as successful completion frequently leads to promotion or preferment, as well as being a matter of individual pride.

However, one of the less attractive features of Japanese society, to the western observer at least, is its domination by men and the relatively low priority which it accords to the education and training of women. As a result, with few exceptions, however able and well-qualified academically women may be, they remain outside the mainstream of Japanese industrial and public career opportunities. Where they are employed by large corporations, they are often treated as temporary employees and expected before long to marry and leave the company. Many women work for smaller, less prestigious companies where they receive lower salaries than men, have less job security and less opportunity for training or educational development. To a considerable extent, the Japanese executive's ability and willingness to dedicate himself to his company depends upon a willingness on the part of his wife to forsake a career for herself and concentrate upon maintaining a house and raising children.

However, while it would seem that for the vast majority of Japanese women, marriage and child-bearing remain life's principal objectives, there is an increasing minority of younger women, especially among university graduates, whose aspirations extend beyond the home into a career. Moreover, the government recognising these legitimate aspirations, introduced recently an Equal Employment Opportunities Law, which has encouraged some companies to recruit more women university graduates for posts of equal status to those available to men. In addition, new maternity leave arrangements make it easier for women in jobs to retain them after child-birth. However, there are strong cultural pressures still making it difficult for women to pursue careers on equal footing with men and many women themselves prefer not to seek out senior positions but are content with jobs of lower status and salary which at least are free from the long working hours and considerable pressures inevitable in managerial posts in Japan.

The educational background

From a governmental point of view, Japan, is, by British standards, a highly centralised society. Although, for administrative purposes, the country is divided into municipalities and prefectures, roughly equivalent to British metropolitan districts and shire counties, and individual Japanese take pride in their allegiance to individual prefectures, nevertheless the writ of government ministries in Tokyo runs powerfully over the country as a whole. In the case of the school system, for example, the Ministry of Education (the Monbusho) lays down national guidelines for school curricula, in order, as it puts it, 'to ensure an optimum national level of learning, while at the same time adhering to the principle of equal educational opportunity'. In other words, a national curriculum has been a feature of Japanese schools for many years.

For individuals, however, perhaps the most important feature of contemporary Japanese society is its obsession with education. In the words of an American observer of the Japanese educational scene, 'It would be difficult to identify a country with a greater historical or contemporary zest for learning than Japan'.[6] This obsession manifests itself in a fiercely competitive educational system, starting at kindergarten, proceeding through nine years of compulsory elementary and lower secondary school from age 6 to 15, and then on through upper secondary school (15 to 18) to university, junior college, or post-secondary vocational institution (see Figure 1.1). Thus, although the structure of the education system closely mirrors that of the United States, having been imposed on the country shortly after the war by the American occupation forces, in spirit and practice it is very different. Japanese schools have a very demanding curriculum, prescribed for them by the Ministry of Education, and in order to follow it they are required to operate an educational programme for at least 240 days each year. In most cases, therefore, children attend school six days a week for over forty weeks a year and are thus required to spend more time at school than in virtually any other country in the world. During their years of schooling, Japanese children achieve high levels of accomplishment in their native language and in mathematics, and acquire habits of diligence and perseverance which, in Duke's view, and that of many other observers of the Japanese scene, equip them extremely well as 'future workers'.[7]

In order for students to enter the elite post-secondary institutions, which are themselves highly calibrated — the most prestigious institution of higher education in Japan is, for example, the University of Tokyo, and within that establishment the most highly-regarded faculty is that of Law — students must obtain high grades in the 'best' elementary school, in order to obtain entry to the 'best' lower secondary school, and so to the 'best' upper secondary school. At lower secondary level, over 96 per cent of the schools are run by local education authorities, so that private schools are relatively uncommon for this age group. They are more numerous, however, at upper secondary level where they constitute about 28 per cent of all the schools. However, some of the most highly regarded schools are six-year privately run secondary schools which span the age range of both lower and upper secondary schools.[8] Such schools, which cater for only a tiny minority of Japanese children, are rather like English public schools, and the competition to enter them is very fierce. The students in these schools compete for the limited number of places in the elite universitites, and study extremely hard to

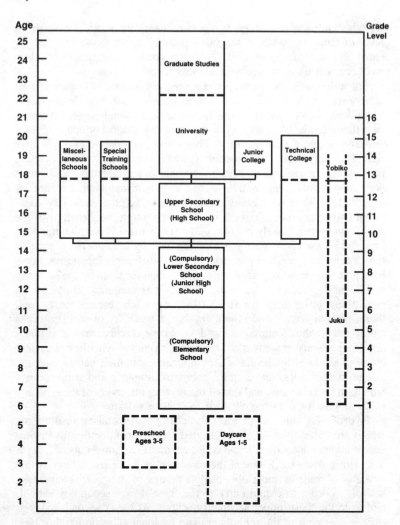

Figure 1.1 The educational system in Japan

prepare for university entrance exams. There are no national examinations for entry into higher education; instead, they repeatedly take mock examinations which are specially prepared by companies which specialise in their production. The results of these examinations are scored by computer and sent to the students and their parents so that they know exactly where they stand in comparison to other children and how good, or bad, their chances are of getting into one of the top universities. Entry into university is determined by a system of vigorous entrance examinations, popularly known as 'examination hell'. This consists of two stages: a one-day standard university examination given throughout the country; and a two or three day's examination set by individual universities and covering perhaps as many as eight different subject areas. A place in the best universities offers the best career prospects, usually with one of the great industrial corporations, or with one of the ministries of state. To secure these advantages for their children, Japanese parents are prepared to spend heavily on their children's education.

In many ways, the most notable development in Japanese education in recent years has been the considerable rate of expansion of post-compulsory education, that is beyond the age of 15. For some years now, about 94 per cent of all Japanese youngsters have stayed on in full-time education until the age of 18, paid for by their parents as only the years of compulsory education are free. In the upper secondary schools parents have to pay fees which represent part only of the costs of schooling. In the state schools fees are, by Japanese standards, relatively moderate, and are somewhat greater in private schools, which themselves receive government subsidies amounting to about half of the teachers' salaries. Moreover, in order to help their children perform well at school, many parents of upper secondary school children send them to private 'cramming' academies, known as *juku* and *yobiko*, for two or three evenings a week for up to four hours a time. Throughout the school system, whether public or private, the emphasis is on rote learning; the role of the teacher is dominant and the curriculum is dominated by the acquisition of subject knowledge with a view to good performance in student tests. Students are 'socialised' very early on in their school career, rarely to question the views of their teachers, and are judged by the ability to memorise facts and concepts.

For the vast majority who stay on at school after 15, two types of high school are available: general and vocational. In 1985 just over 72 per cent of students attended general or academic high schools which, as the term implies, offer non-vocational courses. However, to complicate the picture somewhat, a number of academic high schools offer both general and vocational courses. They are also more prestigious and cater for the more able who mostly aspire to proceed to higher education. Just over 27 per cent of 15- to 18- year-olds, however, attend vocational high schools which concentrate on mainly job-oriented programmes in such areas as accountancy, office work, design, information technology, and agriculture. Significantly, the directly vocational content of these school courses is being steadily reduced as a matter of government policy and, unsurprisingly, the percentage of youngsters attending these courses has declined steadily in the last decade, from 40 per cent in the mid-1970s to 27 per cent a year or two ago. Nevertheless, the vocational secondary schools clearly play an important part in training personnel for Japanese industry and business, at what can broadly by described as technician and craft levels, and we shall examine their role in more detail later.

All upper secondary schools, as throughout the Japanese school system, are what we would describe as 'comprehensive', in that they cater for a wide ability range. Indeed, selection or streaming within schools seems to be abhorred and, as far as could be ascertained, not only the form of curriculum but similar teaching methods and materials are used for all students. On the other hand, there is clearly a differentiation between schools, not just between general and vocational secondary schools: in any given locality certain schools, whether public or private, will be more highly sought after, especially those which are regarded as providing an acknowledged route into the better institutions of higher education. These schools will have a very competitive entry examination and, for all the reasons we are familiar with in this country, tend to recruit a substantial proportion of their students from professional and other highly-placed socioeconomic groups. There are also, inevitably, considerable differences in standard between different parts of the country, with the greatest differences between the towns, which attract the best teachers, very highly paid incidentally by British standards, and the remoter rural areas.

Everywhere, however, the educational system is intensely meritocratic, with students placed under increasing pressure to succeed, both by society at large and by their parents in particular. Although one result of this pressure is relatively high academic standards — for example, the mathematical ability displayed by the average Japanese school-leaver is probably the highest in the world[9] — it also has its obverse and dark side. The very strong cultural pressure put upon students is inevitably accompanied by relatively high rates of stress-related illnesses, resulting in a degree of truancy, violence and, at worst, suicide among Japanese students. Although juvenile crime and delinquency are relatively low compared with other industrial nations, and, generally speaking, Japanese youths still have high aspirations and morale, there is evidence of growing dissatisfaction with the highly competitive educational system. This dissatisfaction is also linked to the concern that the present system does not encourage divergent, creative thinking and imagination, qualities that will be increasingly important in a society dominated by information technology.

These concerns led the previous Prime Minister, Mr Nakasone, to set up an *ad hoc* National Council on Educational Reform directly responsible to him, to put forward proposals for educational reform and to report within a fixed time-scale. To date, four major reports have appeared on the educational system[10] and they offer a trenchant analysis which criticises its narrowness of outlook, pursuit of uniformity, outdated curricula and teaching methods and, in general, its failure to equip pupils for contemporary society. However, given the conservative nature of Japanese society, and the deeply-entrenched attitudes of the great majority of parents, it is doubtful if radical reform will occur in the near future. Indeed, there is some doubt if the political will to bring it about really exists.

Having completed three years at their upper secondary school, a substantial proportion of 18-year-olds then move on to some form of post-secondary education or training. Over 35 per cent attend four-year university or two-year junior college courses, a proportion which has more than doubled since 1965. There are no fewer than 460 universities, of very varying standards, in Japan, catering for over 1,840,000 students, of whom more than three-quarters are men, and 73 per cent are enrolled in private institutions. Paradoxically, the rigour which dominates academic study in Japanese schools is largely absent where undergraduates are concerned. Having obtained a university place, it is very difficult for a student to lose it, even though he or she may attend few classes and pass few courses. This resting on one's laurels is popularly known as the 'moratorium' and does at least have the virtue of allowing the student, who has emerged from 'examination hell', to enter university, and who upon graduation and the securing of a job will devote himself largely to his corporation, the opportunity of psychologically letting off steam. The 536 two-year junior colleges cater for about 380,000 students, of whom almost 90 per cent are women and 90 per cent are enrolled in private institutions. Most of these colleges offer what are termed 'women's courses' in such subjects as home economics, education and nursing. In addition, they offer programmes in traditional female subjects such as flower arranging, the tea ceremony and, so we are solemnly assured in one institution, humility. In these respects, they are not so much academic institutions in the West European sense, as finishing schools, whose purpose is to enhance the marriage prospects of young women.

In addition to the 35 per cent of the age-group who attend universitites and junior colleges, approximately a further 20 per cent attend special training or miscellaneous schools — vocational training institutions whose role will be examined in detail later in the chapter. Finally, there is a strictly limited number of technical colleges which straddle the secondary/post-secondary divide as they recruit youngsters at 15 and offer them five-year courses, thus retaining them until the age of 20. These institutions, too, will be discussed further.

To sum up, it will be seen that the vast majority of Japanese youngsters stay on at school until they are 18 and during their schooling the greater proportion receive little or no vocational education. Within the secondary school system, the emphasis is on the desirability of providing a general education, and this is accepted by industrial and public training centres as a firm foundation on which to build. Thus there is no pressure to include a substantial vocational element for all in secondary education, and one conclusion to be drawn is that an effective way of providing a highly-trained work force is to ensure that they have a solid basis of general education upon which to erect a structure of vocational training. This, in turn, depends upon the commitment of Japanese parents to the long-term education of their children, and their willingness to invest a considerable proportion of their income in it.

The provision of vocational education and training

As has already been described, the lion's share of vocational education and training, some three-quarters, is provided by industry. Of the other quarter, some is provided by educational establishments, public or private, approved by the Ministry of Education; and some is made available by institutions run or approved by the Ministry of Labour; the former comprise vocational courses in upper secondary schools, technical colleges, and special training and miscellaneous schools, and the latter consist of vocational training centres, vocational training colleges and skill development centres (see Figure 1.2). In addition, the Ministry of Labour runs the Institute of Vocational Training which plays a very important role in training instructors for both public and private institutions, and also for industry. It is to these institutions that we shall first turn our attention.

As we have seen, courses in vocational education and training are provided within the education system principally by *Secondary Vocational Schools*, that is upper secondary schools catering for the 15 to 18 age range; most of these schools offer exclusively vocational courses, while others offer both vocational and general courses. To complicate the situation further, upper secondary school courses are available on the basis of part-time study, and by correspondence, in which case they last for four years or more. However, as one would expect, the vast majority of students, approximately 95 per cent in 1984, undertake full-time courses and it is upon these that we shall concentrate.[11] In all, they cater for about 27 per cent of the relevant age group, comprising about 1,400,000 students in 1984. By and large, these students are of lower academic ability than those taking general courses, but within individual vocational schools there may be quite a wide range of ability, so that it would be a mistake to assume that these students come solely, or even principally, from the lower half of the ability range. Indeed, while the general schools cater, on average, for students of higher ability, they

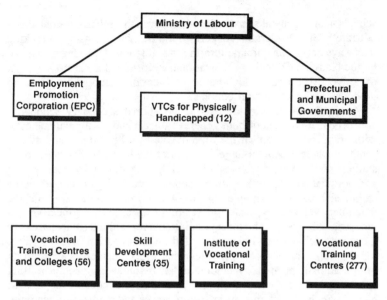

Figure 1.2 Public vocational training in Japan (1985)

also accept students from the bottom of the ability range. In both cases, there are considerable differences in mean student ability both between one school and another in a given municipality or prefecture, and also between one part of the country and another. A typical Secondary Vocational School in the Tokyo area, for example, has a roll of about 950 students, of whom only 13 are girls. Thus, just over 300 are admitted each year and, of these 20 per cent come in on the recommendation of their junior high schools, the other 80 per cent via an entrance examination sat by all Tokyo candidates for Senior High Schools on the same day. This particular Secondary Vocational School cannot afford to be too rigorous in its selection as there are usually only as many applicants as there are places.

Vocational schools and courses are classified into six major fields: technical (or industrial), commercial, agriculture, fisheries, home economics, and nursing. By far the largest number of students are undertaking either technical or commercial courses: about 490,000 on the former, very largely consisting of boys; and 560,000 on the latter, mainly girls. As might be expected, the vast majority of students complete their courses: in upper secondary schools as a whole, in 1983 only about 2.4 per cent did not do so, though the percentage was higher in vocational schools than in general schools. However, even this relatively small drop-out rate is of considerable concern to the Monbusho, who are looking into ways and means of ameliorating the situation. One idea canvassed by the National Council on Educational Reform is that, in the selection of university entrants, favourable consideration should be given to graduates from vocational courses.

As far as the curriculum of the vocational secondary schools is concerned, it consists of both general subjects and vocational subjects, with about 60 per cent of the time devoted to the former, and 40 per cent to the latter. General subjects comprise the Japanese language; social studies; mathematics; science; a foreign language, usually English; art; and physical education. Vocational subjects are fairly specialised: in the technical area, for example, the most important specialisms include machinery, electricity, electronics, architecture, civil engineering and industrial chemistry. The most popular courses in the technical area are those in machinery and electricity and an examination of the former, for example, shows that it provides what Prais[12] describes as 'training in operational specifics', including detailed studies of types of milling cutters and of gear-wheels. Similarly, commercial courses, dominated by girls, include such matters as trial balances and methods of depreciation. The content of the vocational part of the courses is, therefore, quite job specific, also illustrated by the fact that students, before they complete their courses, can take the highly specialised trade tests, to which we have referred earlier, in such areas as boiler technician, gas-welding technician, book-keeping, and licensed information processing technician. At the same time the courses cover a relatively broad vocational front: a typical business studies course, for example, includes typing, double-entry book-keeping, commercial law, marketing, and basic electronic data processing. As Prais points out, this represents a broader mix than is normally found in commercial courses in the United Kingdom, and students who enter employment having completed the course would normally expect to receive training from the company that employs them. However, specific courses in data processing and computer science are available in special training schools for slightly older students, aged 18 to 20. In general, personal observation would suggest that the vocational schools are well equipped, in the case of both technical and commercial subjects, for example, with the latest equipment.

It is clear, therefore, that in comparing Japanese vocational courses at this level with comparable courses offered in British non-advanced further education, the former comprise a much broader curriculum, both with their mix of general and vocational subjects and also across the sweep of vocational studies themselves. They also give greater emphasis to the theoretical bases to practical applications, so providing a foundation for those who wish to move on to higher education. Of great importance is the fact that these courses, roughly comparable in standard to a British Business and Technician Education Council (BTEC) National Diploma, cater for many more students than their English counterparts. The annual output of students, for example, who successfully complete courses in the subject areas of machinery, electrical and electronic engineering and business studies in Japanese vocational secondary schools is of the order of 265,000, while in the United Kingdom the annual output from BTEC and City and Guilds courses in comparable fields is about 24,000. Even allowing for the fact that Japan has a population slightly more than twice that of the United Kingdom, the difference is most marked. Another contrast between the two countries concerns the examination and validation of the courses. Unlike the United Kingdom with its plethora of examining and validating bodies such as BTEC, City and Guilds, and the Royal Society of Arts, Japan has no national bodies of this sort. Instead, each school validates its own courses, on the American model, so that there is probably some variation in standard from one school to another.

On the other hand, having successfully completed a vocational course, those who wish to enter a job immediately have little difficulty in obtaining a suitable post. This may be either with a large firm or corporation, which requires them then to undertake their own training programmes, or with the smaller firms who find it more difficult to provide specialised training, and so rely more heavily on the vocational education and training provided by the schools. In addition, a proportion will take a further course of vocational education and training, either in the increasingly popular special training schools or in a junior college or university. In a typical graduating class of about 310 in a Tokyo vocational high school, some 250 go straight into jobs which they choose from about 1,300 offers, 20 enter university or junior college, 20 enter special training schools, and 20 take a year off to prepare for and resit their university entrance.

In general, secondary vocational schools seem reasonably successful in providing courses which combine general education with broadly-based vocational training. While for many students they may not impart immediately useable skills, they do provide a foundation upon which industrial training, provided by industry itself, can build. On the other hand, as we have seen, the proportion of students undertaking vocational courses in the upper secondary schools has steadily declined due to lack of student demand. The schools are seen in parents' eyes as inferior to the general schools and morale in them has undoubtedly suffered. Partly for this reason, they have found it difficult to recruit sufficient numbers of good teachers of vocational subjects, a phenomenon that is by no means restricted to Japan but is common to similar institutions throughout the developed world.

In addition to the secondary vocational schools, the Ministry of Education is also concerned with vocational education and training in two other types of institutions, technical colleges and special training schools. There are currently only sixty-two *Technical Colleges* in Japan, and there are no plans to increase their number. The system of technical colleges, or colleges of technology as some of them prefer to call themselves, was officially established in 1961, and their purpose was to help meet the needs of expanding Japanese industry by training what are termed 'promising men with higher technological ability'[13] in specific vocational areas. And, indeed, they do almost exclusively recruit young men: of the 46,000 students attending them in 1984, only just over 1,500 were girls. Of the 62 technical colleges scattered all over Japan, 58 are public institutions, 54 of them being run directly by the Monbusho and 4 by prefectures, and only 4 are private. Of the total of 62, 54 are designated as technical colleges, concentrating very largely on engineering, 5 are mercantile marine colleges and 3 offer courses in radio communication. Virtually every technical college has departments of mechanical and electrical engineering, and many have departments of chemical engineering, civil engineering and agricultural engineering. Although, as we have seen, the government has no plans to establish more colleges, it is intended that some new departments will be added to existing technical colleges to meet national needs: during 1986–7, for example, it was proposed to create five departments of Information Technology.

The technical colleges recruit boys who have completed their junior secondary school courses and offer them a five-year programme which they claim is of a sufficiently high quality to ensure that their graduates have acquired knowledge and practical skills in their vocational specialisms almost on the same level as university graduates. In keeping with the Japanese philosophy of vocational education and training within the educational system, students in the colleges are required to devote a proportion of their time to general education. As the prospectus of the Tokyo National College of Technology, one of the leading technical colleges, puts it, 'Needless to say, to acquire a wide knowledge of general subjects is required for building up a creative man of technology'. To this end, students study Japanese and foreign languages (English and German), history, law, economics, music, and art, as well as mathematics, physics, and chemistry, as bases for their vocational studies. The latter are highly specific and wide ranging and the colleges appear to be very well equipped with a wide range of up-to-date machinery.

Students pay relatively low fees, as the vast majority of the cost of running the colleges is met from government funds. If the Tokyo National College of Technology is anything to go by, competition for places is quite severe, there is a very low drop-out rate, and virtually all students complete their courses, and on graduation have no difficulty in finding jobs. Indeed, the colleges claim that their students fare better in this respect than the products of the special training schools. A small proportion of graduates move into university courses and, as a rule, are admitted through examination into the third year of a related university department of technology. A substantial proportion of those obtaining university places do so in one of Japan's two technological universities, at Nagaoka, about 300 kilometres north of Tokyo, and at Toyohashi, about 250 kilometres west of Tokyo, both established in 1976.

To outward appearances, the technical colleges are successful and produce well-trained graduates who are much sought after by industry. However, as we have seen, they are relatively few in number and there are no plans to add to them. Officially it is stated that this is largely because there is no great demand for them from parents or students. A contributory reason may be that they require students to commit themselves to a relatively narrow vocational specialism at 15 and this is too young an age at which to do so. Moreover, although some of the colleges claim that their products are technologists rather than technicians, and that they have the same chance of rising to senior management positions as university graduates, this may not be true of all of them, and there is reason to believe that many of their graduates have to content themselves with lower level posts.

Far more numerous than the technical colleges as providers of vocational education and training though, unlike them, very largely privately run, are the *Special Training Schools* and *Miscellaneous Schools*. Together, they comprise over 7,300 institutions catering for more than 1,100,000 students. Until 1976 they were all known as miscellaneous schools (or *kakushu gakko*), but in that year the Ministry of Education introduced the new category of special training schools (or *senshu gakko*), in order to promote and enhance this type of provision. To qualify as a special training school, the institution has to meet certain Ministry of Education requirements: for example, their courses have to be of at least one year's duration, though in practice they are usually two years and sometimes three years; the minimum number of hours spent in classroom or lecture-room by day-time students must be 800 hours a year; and the number and qualifications of teaching staff and the provision of facilities must conform to certain specifications. In the decade or so since then, the number of special training schools has grown very considerably so that, in 1986, there were 3,089 of them catering for over 587,000 students.

To deal briefly with the miscellaneous schools first: there are about 4,300 of them enrolling about 530,000 students. They offer courses in a wide range of vocational subjects such as automobile driving, book-keeping, dressmaking (both Japanese and western), cooking, foreign languages, and the use of the abacus which is still widely employed in

17

Japan. However, about one-third of their students, the biggest single group, are undertaking preparatory courses of study for university entrance examinations. The length of courses at miscellaneous schools varies considerably, depending on the subject, but they are usually of one year or more.

Of more significance to the vocational training of Japanese youngsters today are the special training schools.[14] They recruit the great majority of their students at age 18 having graduated from upper secondary schools, and offer them courses in eight fields: technology, agriculture, para-medical subjects, business, health, education and welfare, home economics, and cultural education. Each of the eight fields covers many specific areas of study, and in a given school there will be a number of small departments covering these areas. Technology, for example, includes not only engineering of different kinds, but also construction, electrical and electronic work, wireless communication, automobile mechanics, aviation, shipbuilding and printing; while business includes secretarial work, hotel management, and tourism.

Of the total of 3,089 special training schools, almost 90 per cent are privately owned or run by individuals or corporations, and their 587,000 students are 56 per cent female and 44 per cent male. Their popularity has greatly increased in recent years because they seem to offer better prospects of employment than a general course in a university or junior college. They also free their students from the prospect of the 'examination hell' which entry to the latter entails. With higher living standards, more parents can now afford their fees and, for young men in particular, they offer one of the few avenues outside direct employment of obtaining job-specific vocational training.

The schools themselves are also very responsive to market demands and can, and do, introduce courses in subject areas in which their graduates are likely to find employment. Two of the growth areas in recent years, for example, are computer studies and business studies. Moreover, as there are no national examining bodies like the British Business and Technician Council and City and Guilds, they can rapidly adapt course content to the perceived needs of employers. However, a national system of certification or licensing has now grown up which provides a broad framework for many courses. As many employers expect their potential employees to have obtained a certificate or licence, so the schools now increasingly prepare their students to take them. They are obtained by successfully passing examinations run by the national and prefectural governments which, in 1984, covered more than 600 subjects. They are particularly important in the newer service and information technology industries and new occupations such as energy conservation and health and welfare where employees will not be taken on, or promoted, unless they hold the appropriate licence.

Inevitably, among so many special training schools, only loosely subject to Ministry of Education supervision, standards of training vary considerably. Some of them are more concerned with making a profit than training their students properly, in some the standard of teaching is inadequate, and in others there is insufficient, outdated equipment. Nevertheless, in general they offer a sound form of vocational training, and undoubtedly they have been increasingly successful in recent years, attracting more and more students who seem to find little difficulty in finding employment. Certainly, as together with the miscellaneous schools their student population is now in excess of 1,100,000, they make a major contribution to the training of Japan's skilled personnel. Moreover, as they are very largely privately run, they illustrate the key role played by the private sector in the Japanese system of vocational education and training.

As far as the provision of vocational education and training outside the educational system is concerned, as we have observed, the majority of such training is offered by industry itself. There are, however, state-sponsored training facilities which are run partly by the national government, and partly by the prefectural governments. Both these forms of provision are governed by the principles laid down by the Vocational Training Law of 1969 and its subsequent amendments,[15] the most recent of which is the Human Resources Development Law of 1985, which lays particular stress on the importance of retraining and the updating of skills. As a consequence of this law, the term 'vocational training' is being superseded, in Ministry of Labour circles at least, by that of 'human resources development'. Broadly speaking, the law enunciates two main principles: that sufficient provision of training opportunities should be available to meet the needs of individual workers arising at all stages of their occupational life; and the provision of training should both take into account changes in industrial technology and the employment market, and should also properly evaluate and recognise the occupational capabilities of workers. The law emphasises that while the primary responsibility for providing suitable and sufficient training rests with the employers, both national and local governments will provide a good deal of assistance and encouragement.

The law further identifies three main priority areas of vocational education and training. These are initial training for young people about to enter the world of work; upgrading training to impart additional skills to those in work; and what is given the long-winded term 'occupational capacity redevelopment training', namely, retraining for workers who wish to or are forced to change their jobs. In keeping with the Japanese system of close central regulation of matters pertaining to education and training, the three types of training described above are classified into courses for the various trades and occupations, and the Ministry of Labour lays down standards or guidelines for each course. These relate to such matters as curricula, the duration of training, and the necessary facilities and equipment. Public vocational training institutions have to meet these specifications in their programmes while those operated by industry are deemed to be 'authorized' if they do so. In that case, they qualify for various forms of public subsidy and assistance. As these standards are quite flexible, industry finds it both reasonably straightforward and also profitable to meet them and, as a result, there were about 1,300 authorized training projects run by various industrial organizations in the earlier part of the decade.[16]

The responsibility, then, for the public provison of vocational training, lies ultimately with the Ministry of Labour which has the responsibility of drawing up a national, five-year basic vocational training plan, which is part and parcel of the national economic development plan. The five-year plan — the country is currently in the middle of its Fourth Basic Vocational Training Plan which runs from 1986 to 1990 — is designed to specify the trends in the demands for skilled labour and to make plans to meet those demands. One of the most impressive features of the Japanese system of vocational education and training is the systematic way in which these plans are drawn up, including the compilation of an annual survey of skills in short supply which is undertaken by the Ministry through direct mailing to a sample of representative industries. Once the national five-year plan is drawn up, each of the 47 prefectures, through its own vocational training council, is then required to formulate plans for its own locality. In the case of Kanagawa Prefecture, for example, which includes the south-western part of Tokyo, the town of Yokohama with a population of over three million, and the nearby countryside, it very thoroughly examines its training needs by surveying all firms in the Prefecture and by commissioning a prestigious 'Think Tank' to prepare a report on training courses likely to be needed in the immediate future as a result of industrial and technological developments. Equally impressive is the manner in which the Prefecture has rapidly proceeded to introduce new courses into some of its training institutions in such areas as Mechatronics — the application of electronics to mechanical engineering — and Computer-Aided Graphic Design.

In its oversight of Japan's system of vocational education and training, the Ministry of Labour operates through two subsidiary bodies, The Employment Promotion Corporation (EPC) and the Japanese Vocational Ability Development Association (JAVDA). The EPC's relation to the Ministry is not unlike that of the Manpower Services Commission to the Department of Employment in the United Kingdom, though it seems to be more directly under the Ministry's control than its British equivalent. Its chief functions are to run the national training institutions and to receive and pass judgement on major bids for financial assistance from firms for training help. Thus, it encourages private sector employers, either individually or jointly, to institute and develop training and retraining schemes by making grants and subsidies, especially to small and medium-sized companies, and by making loans for the installation of vocational training facilities. JAVDA, which like the EPC is based in Tokyo, was established in 1974, together with forty-seven local branches in each of the prefectures. Its main functions include assisting firms with their training, especially by helping medium-sized and small firms to set up co-operative training facilities, supplying training materials and information, undertaking research into training methods, and running the national system of trade skill testing. As a result of the Human Resources Development Act of 1985, another branch of the Ministry of Labour, the Human Resources Development Administration, is charged with the particular responsibility of improving the skills of workers throughout their professional life as part of the national recognition of the need to organize vocational training as a continuous process made available throughout the employee's career.

As we have seen, the training is provided partly in public institutions, and mainly in industry, in the ratio of approximately one to three. If we look first at the former, it will be seen that they consist of some institutions which are run by the Ministry of Labour itself, through the EPC, and a substantially larger number which are run by the Prefectural and municipal governments (see Figure 1.2). In 1985, the Ministry of Labour operated 91 institutions, 56 of which were *Vocational Training Centres* (VTCs) or colleges and the other 35 *Skill Development Centres* (SDCs).[17] The difference between them is that originally the VTCs concentrated largely on basic vocational training for school leavers, while the SDCs offered retraining and up-dating courses for adults. However, as the former are increasingly concerned with adult provision, the distinctions between them seem to have become largely eroded. Together, the 91 institutions turn out annually over 150,000 trainees. In addition, the EPC runs the very important Institute of Vocational Training, which trains instructors, an establishment which will be examined in detail later. Also, the national government, though in this case not through the EPC, runs twelve vocational training centres specifically for the physically handicapped. The prefectural and municipal governments together operate substantially more institutions than the EPC, numbering 277 in 1985, of which six were specifically for physically handicapped trainees. However, as individual prefectural institutions are smaller than those operated by the EPC, their annual output is about 180,000. In other words, the total output of these types of institution together is of the order of 330,000 a year, a significant contribution to Japan's stock of trained men and women.

As we have seen, the public training system has two main aims: to

21

provide basic training for school-leavers, and to retrain and up-date adult workers. However, in recent years the VTCs have experienced a sharp decline in demand from school-leavers, who at 18 are increasingly turning to the special training schools for their vocational training. There is, of course, a small percentage who leave school at 15, many of them at the lower end of the ability range, some of whom enter VTCs. Inevitably, this group tend to have low self-esteem and are often resentful of their 'failure' in the eyes of society at large. Some of the VTCs catering for this age group are small and offer courses at a fairly low-level in premises that are sometimes lacking in equipment and facilities. However, the majority of VTCs offering basic training recruit senior high school leavers at age 18 and, from my own observation at least, operate in reasonable and well-equipped premises that compare very favourably with a British technical college, for example. In any case, with the smaller number of school-leavers coming forward, and an increasing need for adult up-dating and retraining, they are more and more concentrating on the latter. The only major exception is in such subject areas as Mechatronics in which, because of the expensive equipment required, the private sector finds difficulty in providing courses. In the area of adult retraining, increasing emphasis is being placed on the training of women who wish to re-enter the world of work when their children are old enough. In a prefecture on the edge of Tokyo, for example, no fewer than 40 per cent of trainees are women, mainly taking courses in commerce, fashion, and catering.

A typical example of an EPC-run vocational training centre is that at Saitama, on the northern edge of the Tokyo conurbation. A relatively small VTC as EPC-managed centres go, it has about 270 trainees, the great majority of whom are on retraining courses. Most of them come from the immediate hinterland, and are sent by the Japanese equivalent of a Job Centre with a certificate registering them as unemployed, and with a grant which they receive personally from the Ministry of Labour. A typical retraining course lasts one-year full-time, for fifty weeks a year, with only 2 weeks holiday, for five-and-a-half days a week. Most of the students are men taking courses in engineering subjects, but there are also women on a dressmaking course. There are no pre-requirements or educational qualifications needed, and the courses emphasise practical skills. The equipment seems plentiful and up to date, the methods of instruction are practical and straightforward, and virtually all the trainees were finding employment on completion of their courses. In addition, the Saitama VTC offers upgrading courses for people already in employment who wish to improve their skills. These courses last anything from two days to three months, and a condition of entry is that the trainees return to their places of employment on completion of the programme. The main aim of these updating courses is to concentrate skill-training in as short a period as possible, so that small and medium-sized firms can avail themselves of them. Of the twenty-seven or so instructors in the centre, one-third were trained in the Institute of Vocational Training, one-third were university graduates with a year or more of industrial experience, and the rest came directly from industry having successfully completed a required national skill-instructor's examination.

Typical of the more numerous municipal and prefectural voctional training centres are those run by the Kanagawa Prefecture. In all they number thirteen, including one specifically for disabled students. Together they offer approximately 11,000 training places: of these, some 1,200 are for school-leavers, the majority entering at 18 from senior high schools; about 1,350 are for adults undertaking mid-career retraining courses; and about 8,500 are for people in employment taking upgrading skill courses. As everywhere in Japan, the public training system is having to come to grips with the problems of an ageing society, and the increasing rapidity with which skills are becoming obsolescent.

Among the Kanagawa VTCs is one exclusively for women, in an old, rather gloomy building, near the centre of Yokohama. It offers couses in four main areas: industrial catering; welfare, for trainees who will work mainly in old people's homes; in typing, mainly the fiendishly difficult Japanese typewriting, together with some word processing and telexing; and in business management, principally book-keeping and accounting. The first three areas are mainly for older women wishing to return to work, and the fourth is for 18-year old senior high school graduates. The centre has plans to introduce new courses in existing subject areas, such as computing into business management, and also to admit men to the industrial catering courses. The centre's 'graduates' have little or no difficulty in obtaining jobs, especially as many employers prefer the VTC products to those of the private sector as their standards are less variable.

Another, sharply contrasting, Kanagawa VTC, is in a far-flung suburb of Yokohama, in a relatively new building into which it moved from the centre of the city in 1974. In addition to long-standing courses in business skills and western dressmaking (a term which is used to distinguish it from kimono-making courses), it has more recently added computing, and textile and graphic design, and within the past year computer-aided graphic design. It takes in about 230 students a year, from three times as many applicants, mostly at the age of 18, and is a well run, very lively institution, not unlike a good British College of Art specialising in fashion and textile design. It is well equipped with computers and computer-aided design equipment and, on the day I visited it, was full of lively, interested students putting together an impressive fashion show of western clothes for the centre's annual festival or open day. Its 'graduates', like those in the other

VTCs, seemed to have no difficulty in finding employment.

Finally, mention must be made of the *Institute of Vocational Training*, which plays a key role in training instructors of vocational subjects, both for public institutions and for industry. One visiting British group described it as 'in many ways the jewel in the crown of the provision made for vocational training under the auspices of the Ministry of Labour', and, indeed, they were so taken with it that they recommended the establishment of a comparable institution in the United Kingdom.

The institute occupies an impressive site in Sagamihara City, on the western edge of Tokyo, over an hour's ride by underground and train from the centre of the city. Very well equipped with very modern equipment, it also has residential accommodation for its students whom it draws from all over Japan. It has four main functions: to offer initial training courses to would-be vocational instructors; to provide upgrading training courses for practising instructors, both at the institute and by means of correspondence courses; to provide programmes for overseas instructors from the developing world and to train Japanese technical experts to work overseas; and, through its Research and Development Institute, to undertake and disseminate research into various aspects of technical training.[19] Its main function is, however, the first one, namely to offer initial training to instructors, both for the public vocational training institutions and also for authorized training centres in industry. Such instructors are required to possess a licence for the trade they teach issued by the Ministry of Labour, and courses leading to the licence are provided exclusively by the institute. They are of two types: a 'long' course of four years, for 18-year-olds from senior high schools; and 'short' courses of six months for skilled tradesmen with industrial experience, who are employed in industry and are released to undertake the course to qualify them as instructors in their own firms. The 'long' course provides for about 240 young people a year, almost all male, who are admitted through a highly competitive examination. The content of the course includes both specialist vocational study in such areas of engineering as mechanical, electronic — including information technology — electrical, chemical and metallic, as well as in building and wood technology, and also general and cultural subjects. The course contains only a very short industrial placement and the only 'teaching practice' is a relatively short period in the final year, which is spent in a vocational training centre. The annual output from this course is between 220 and 230, of whom some 60 per cent go into public institutions and the remaining 40 per cent into training centres in industry. In recent years the proportion entering public institutions has declined, apparently because there is less demand for them. The 'short' courses are designed for twelve trades ranging from automobile maintenance through sheet-metal processing to plumbing, and the curriculum also includes some pedagogical study. In addition, the institute organises updating training programmes, of anything from three days to six months, for instructors already employed in vocational training. Finally, the research and curriculum development function is an extremely important one and is performed by its own Research and Development Insitute. Among other things, it produces textbooks for use in vocational training institutions throughout the country, it develops video tapes for retraining adults, and it publishes regular bulletins of its research activities together with a bi-monthly technical journal, and sponsors an annual technical conference.

Clearly, the Institute of Vocational Training is of critical importance to the Japanese system of vocational eduction and training. Not only does it produce high quality instructors for both public sector and industrial training centres throughout the country, and promote new teaching materials and methods, but it also provides a focal point for the promotion of sound vocational training across Japan. It is estimated that about 10 per cent of all VTC instructors are products of the institute. Significantly, it is run by the Ministry of Labour and in this respect, as in others, it has no equivalent in Britain.

Vocational training in industry

As we have seen, some three-quarters of Japanese vocational training is provided by industry itself. Just how much industry spends on such training it is impossible to say as no precise information is available but, at least as far as the major companies are concerned, it is very considerable, and substantially more than that spent by comparable British companies. As Ishikawa points out,[20] Japanese employers are generally very committed to the recruitment, training, and preservation of a work force responsive to the present and future needs of their businesses. As a consequence, each of the big companies, as well as many of the smaller ones, develops its own strategy plans and programmes of training so that the picture presented by the Japanese training system within industry is a very complex one and not easily comprehended by the outsider. However, some general features of that system can be highlighted.

First, the Japanese conception of what they describe as 'skill formation', is somewhat different from what in the West would normally be described as 'vocational training'. The Japanese concept of skill formation is what G.W. Ford, an Australian authority on the subject, calls an 'holistic' one,[21] in that it embraces the ideas of education, training, experience and personal development. Indeed, in their training programmes, Japanese companies use the word 'education' a great deal, by which thay mean the development of a highly-educated, skilled, adaptable, flexible and innovative work force which will participate in, and contribute to, the economic well-being of their companies. Practices vary greatly from company to company but, to varying degrees, they combine 'off-the-job' formal training, with 'on-the-job-learning'. The former takes place in training centres which are provided by the companies themselves. In the case of a large corporation such as Hitachi, for example, they have no fewer than five training institutions of their own: the Hitachi Institute of Technology, in Hitachi City, 80 miles northeast of Tokyo; two Hitachi Technical Colleges, one at Keihin, near Yokohama, and the other in Hitachi City; a productivity training centre, wholly devoted to training staff in methods of increasing productivity, and the Hitachi Comprehensive Management Research Centre, also in Hitachi City. At the Keihin technical college, for example, the company runs initial training courses of fifteen months duration in electronics engineering and software engineering for newly-recruited blue-collar and white-collar workers, drawn straight from senior high school and university respectively, at ages 18 and 22, while at the Management Research Centre, special emphasis is placed on the training of executives at all levels of the Hitachi group of companies. Together with an intensive programme of on-the-job training for all its employees, the total training programme was estimated to cost Hitachi 42 million US dollars at the beginning of the present decade, sufficiently large to classify Hitachi as a major educational institution.[22] Virtually all the large corporations and companies in Japan have similar training institutions — Mitsubishi, for example, has five technical institutes of its own — which provide their employees with a life-long programme of training to assure that their technical knowledge is continually upgraded. In addition, these programmes include such subjects as marketing, company history, company products, company objectives, and research and development techniques. The emphasis on the need to develop company loyalty among employees is one which, while alien in many respects of western observers, nevertheless seems to succeed very well in Japan, where for historical reasons the individual feels a strong collective responsibility to the group, a responsibility which inhibits the expression of individualism which we take for granted.

In the past ten or fifteen years, Japanese companies have placed increasing emphasis on the retraining of their employees to enable them to move into new professional areas. Because of the 'horizontal' nature of many Japanese Corporations whose industrial interests range over a wide range of products, they are able to move employees, once retrained, from one part of the company which may be in recession to another which is flourishing. During the 1970s, the cumulative effect of higher prices and wages induced by the massive increase in the cost of oil, together with industrial changes brought about by technological developments, led Japanese industry to introduce a major programme of retraining which has continued ever since. Thus, it has become quite common to move technicians from mechanical engineering to electronic engineering, hardware technicians to software, and blue-collar workers to white-collar employment.

This policy is made easier by the relative willingness of employees to move, and also by another fundamental aspect of Japanese attitudes to skill training, namely, that instead of classifying the industrial work force in terms of unskilled, semi-skilled and skilled, and to see skills in terms of traditional trades, as is common in The United Kingdom and Australia, for example, Japanese managers regard workers as either skilled or unskilled.[23] Moreover, there is a strong emphasis on the need for all workers to develop their skills and to rotate and change jobs as and when necessary. As restrictive trade practices are virtually unknown, these changes may take various forms: for example, moving a worker from one job to another, either temporarily or permanently, within a particular factory, or to a similar job in another factory, or to a completely different type of job, after, of course, a suitable period of retraining. In various ways, the companies provide incentives, in the form of higher wages, for example, for individual employees to update, upgrade and broaden their qualifications and technical knowledge.

This is done both by off-the-job training, which we have briefly described, and by on-the-job training. The latter, like the former, is a complex subject which takes many forms and varies from company to company; however, there are a number of common features. One of the most important is the significant part played by the supervisor or foreman who is expected to perform a training function as part of his job. Another is the range of training techniques developed by Japanese companies such as group working and multi-skilled work targeting. The former is designed to facilitate the exchange of ideas and information among small, cohesive groups of workers, and to humanise work by developing latent creativity. More recently, group working has adopted the use of the 'key worker' approach whereby one highly-trained person acts as the disseminator of knowledge and new techniques. The second technique, multi-skilled work targeting, aims to avoid narrow specialisation, to encourage the workers' ability to adjust, and to increase their desire to learn more. These and other participative on-the-job activities are common in the great majority of the larger Japanese firms. In so far as it is possible to judge from factory visits, there appears to a be a dedication on the part of the work force to high quality and productivity. Thus, virtually all large companies have staff suggestion schemes which produce a flow of ideas for improvements in manufacturing techniques and products; and faulty workmanship or techniques are regularly discussed in what have been termed 'quality circle' meetings, which are regarded by some companies as part of their continuing education or training process.

Another much-vaunted feature of the Japanese corporations is the so-called 'life-time' employment which they ostensibly guarantee their work force. While this is, indeed, to some extent true, a number of important qualifications must be made. First, it only guarantees employment until the age of 55 or 60, when compulsory retirement takes place, though many retired workers continue to work for the same company by moving down several grades, or find employment, often part-time, elsewhere. Second, only a limited proportion of the total force enjoys this facility, even in the big companies, which one estimate puts at between 30 and 50 per cent of the employees, and another at only 25 per cent. As Japan comes face to face with the problems of an ageing society, so the demand to raise the retirement age grows. Until fairly recently, retirement age was 55; at present, just over half of Japanese companies have raised retirement to 60, though the smaller ones find it difficult to do so because of increased costs. The National Council on Educational Reform has recommended that the retirement age be raised to 65, as is presently the case in one or two companies such as Matsushita, maker of National and Panasonic electronic goods. Whether the target of a retirement age of 65 will eventually be reached is, however, very much open to question.

As we have seen, the higher echelons of the Japanese industry and business are largely the preserve of men, and few if any women are able to obtain top-level jobs. Because of the very high cost of living in Japan, well over half of all married women have some form of full or part-time employment, but almost entirely at the lower levels of industry and frequently with small companies. Where they have young children of school age, married women usually work part-time, usually from about ten in the morning until three o'clock in the afternoon when the children leave school. In April 1986, an Equal Employment Opportunity Act was passed requiring companies to make efforts to avoid sex discrimination in recruiting, hiring, job assignment and promotion, and forbidding discrimination in worker training, dismissal policies, welfare and retirement benefits. In addition, a government arbitration commission was established to which women can take claims of discrimination. However, despite this legislation and the new legal status which it affords Japanese women, discrimination continues largely unabated and it will be a long time, if ever, before women are on an equal footing with men in regard to job opportunities and promotion prospects.

We have concentrated so far on the training activities of the big companies, because they are the most developed and the best known. However, they employ little more than 30 per cent of all Japanese industrial workers, the great majority working in small business and family firms, many of which offer relatively little training. Where training is regarded as important, the companies often employ men and women who have attended courses at the public vocational training centres, or themselves provide various forms of on-the-job training, along the lines of that offered by the big corporations. In addition, with the help of government and prefectural subsidies, many groups of small firms operating in the same geographical location and trade come together to establish their own training centres. Just such a one is the Tatami Mat Training Centre, in Saitama, near Tokyo, where there are numbers of small firms making this particular product. It should not be forgotten that, in addition to modern artefacts like automobiles and electronic products, there is a substantial market in Japan for traditional products such as kimonos and tatami mats. The latter form the flooring of the majority of Japanese houses and consist of rectangular mats made from a special type of grass grown in southern Japan, mainly in the islands of Shikoku and Kyushu. Their manufacture is a highly skilled craft, and although the mats can be made automatically, the process is more expensive. The centre in Saitama is run by the twenty-nine small firms in the Prefecture, with the aid of grants both from the Ministry of Labour and the Prefecture itself, and the craft union is closely involved in its running. The centre is unique in that it offers a full-time three-year course, whereas other tatami mat training centres offer part-time courses only. The trainees who number about twenty-five per year are all male; they are recruited mainly as 18-year-old senior high school graduates, and on the successful completion of the course receive a certificate which enables them to practice their trade, and grants them some exemption for JAVDA trade tests. Apparently they have no difficulty in finding jobs as the mats are still in demand — a typical mat lasts fifteen years before it has to be replaced — and tatami mat craftsmen are in short supply as too few youngsters are undertaking training. Apart from the Principal of the Centre, all the instructors are part-time and are working in the industry in the Saitama area. Another similar training centre, but this time entirely female, is one in Kamakura, a historic city 30 miles south of Tokyo, for the training of kimono-craftswomen. Run by the local industry and approved by the Prefecture, it is one of 120 throughout the country, including about ten in Tokyo. Although the national production of kimonos has declined from about 28 million in the 1970s to about 16 million today, still about one person in ten in Japan buys one every year, and many more rent them, mainly for special occasions, such as funerals and weddings. The centre has 350 women students, mostly married women wanting to augment their husbands' salaries, who undertake part-time courses lasting between four and five years. The students pay no tuition fees and after three months basic training receive a payment for the kimonos they make, which is much less than that received by recognised, and fully qualified, craftwomen. The making of kimonos is highly skilled, and the courses consist mainly of high craft skills, together with 'cultural' subjects such as moral education and civics.

The instructors who all work in the local industry, are required to have a skill Certificate in the making of kimonos, and are licensed as instructors by the Prefecture after a forty-eight hours' training course in one of their own vocational training centres or in the training facilities of an authorised company.

Finally, there is a large number of private agencies throughout Japan which offer to companies and firms at commercial rates training programmes for their use. As is the case in the United Kingdom, where the last few years have witnessed a marked increase in their activities, they concentrate mainly on courses for managerial, supervisory, technical and professional employees across a wide range of subjects. These include personnel management, industrial relations, industrial engineering, quality control, marketing and cost accounting.

Conclusions

Japan's system of vocational education and training is an enormously complex one, and like its educational system is a microcosm of Japanese society, the product of social and cultural values and attitudes, some deeply rooted in Japanese history, and some the product of the country's wartime and post-war experiences. Although, clearly, its system of vocational education and training has made a major contribution to its post-war economic success, not least because it enhances what has been called its 'stock of national competences',[24] it is difficult, if not impossible, to quantify that contribution. As we have seen, the system comprises three main elements: the contribution of the education system, mainly in terms of general education, but also in the form of vocational education in some high schools; vocational education and training provided by the growing number of special training schools, and by the vocational training centres run by the prefectural governments and the Employment and Promotion Corporation under the auspices of the Ministry of Labour; and, third, the great bulk of industrial training provided by industry itself.

There is no doubt that each of these three elements has its role to play, and not least important is the sound basis of general education provided by the country's effective school system. This effectiveness is dependent, to a great extent, on the Japanese obsession with education and the willingness both of Japanese parents to invest considerable amounts of time and money in their children's education and also that of their children to submit themselves to the rigours of the system. However desirable or otherwise these features of Japanese society may be, it is difficult to see how they could be grafted on to the educational system in the United Kingdom or other western countries. As we have seen, the great majority of companies recruit their employees at age 18 or later, and seem content with the general education which their new entrants have received and which they use as a base upon which to erect their own scaffolding of industrial training. To western eyes, there is a marked lack of interplay and liaison between education and industry at either national level, as represented by the Ministries of Education and Labour, or at institutional level. The intercourse between schools and industry which is currently being encouraged in British schools through such initiatives as the Technical and Vocational Education Initiative has little or no parallel in Japanese secondary schools. The reason is mainly because they do not perceive a need for it.

The school system and the system of vocational education and training use similar pedagogic methods, based very largely on rote learning, methods which are increasingly criticised for the deadening effect they have on creativity. Recent technological developments, especially in the field of information technology, require a much more creatively-inclined work force, and there is a growing demand among the big companies for more engineers and technicians capable of forwarding company research and development programmes. The latter development has led some of the country's major companies to establish 'university' courses in their own institutes to which they second their own employees. More generally, the growing realisation of the shortcomings in the country's educational system has fuelled the current drive for increased diversity and creativity as highlighted by the reports of the National Council for Educational Reform. If these reforms should come about, though the esentially conservative nature of Japanese society will make that difficult to achieve, they may bring other problems in their wake. As a recent report indicates,[25] any relaxation in the present tight, conformist system may well erode the very features — standardization, a high level of achievement in a well-defined core of basic skills, and a conformist attitude — which are its strengths. These may also make the future work force of Japan less amenable to the needs and ethos of industry. However, the present system has itself changed a great deal, is very resilient and, if past experience is anything to go by, well able to adapt itself to future needs.

In the area of vocational training, the important part played by the private sector, notably in the shape of the special training schools, is a factor of key importance. Their expansion in recent years is in direct response to parental and student demand and the willingness of industry to employ their products. Whatever their shortcomings may be, as measured by broadly educational and pedagogic criteria, their strength lies in their ability to respond quickly and effectively to perceived market demands. As we have seen, their recent increase is due in part to growing Japanese prosperity which makes it possible for parents to pay their not unsubstantial fees.

The training provided by industry itself, at least in the case of the large corporations, is widespread, intensive, and of high quality. The Japanese have no doubt that investment in human resources, which they see as their most precious capital, is essential to maintain the economic well-being of their country. This is not to say, of course, that the country and the economy are not without their problems. Not least among them is that of their ageing population. Japan's birth-rate has fallen considerably in the last 25 years, and the percentage of young people in the population is steadily diminishing. The resulting labour shortage is to some extent being overcome by the increasing deployment of robots in industrial processes, but these may well bring problems in their wake, especially if eventually they displace substantial numbers of workers and create unemployment. Second, the coming of increasingly sophisticated computers and of radically new communication techniques is creating an 'information society' which requires more creativity and less conformity as technological innovation becomes more difficult. As we have seen, the nature of Japanese vocational education and training inhibits, rather than promotes, the development of creative thinking. Other difficulties faced by the Japanese economy include greatly increased labour costs brought about by the rising value of the yen, intensifying competition from countries such as South Korea, Taiwan and China, and mounting pressure for protectionist policies in key markets in the United States and Western Europe.

However, the Japanese are among the first to acknowledge both the shortcomings in their present system of vocational education and training, and also the challenges it will have to face in the future. Their flexibility and adaptability in coping with equally daunting problems in the recent past suggest that they are well equipped to come to terms with, and surmount, them.

Chapter two

Australia: The Tyranny of Distance

To the British visitor, Australia presents a disconcerting mixture of the familiar and the very different. In education, as in many other facets of Australian life, the British inheritance is patent and expresses itself in administrative structures, institutional terminology, and a keen interest in and, often, a detailed knowledge of British educational developments. Given the strong links between the two countries and the steady stream of Australian educationalists visiting the United Kingdom and *vice versa*, this is perhaps hardly surprising. In many other respects, and often not the most obvious ones, the differences between the two educational systems are substantial, and increasingly divergent. Differences notwithstanding, the warm welcome extended to visitors by Australians and their genuine interest in sharing experiences and insights make a stay in the country a most rewarding experience.

Australia is, above all, a huge country. With an area of over 7,600,000 square kilometres, it is more than thirty times as large as the United Kingdom; thus, the most direct air route between Sydney and Perth, on either side of the continent, spans a distance of 3,200 kilometres, while the most direct route between Darwin in the north and Hobart, the most southern state capital, is even further, at 3,700 kilometres. Although rich in natural resources, such as coal, bauxite, iron ore and uranium, the country has a harsh landscape and, over much of it, a harsh climate, characterised by lack of water. Vast areas are desert or semi-desert, unsuitable for settlement, so that the population is very small compared to its size, approaching sixteen million, or about two people per kilometre. Moreover, Australian society is, and always has been, an urban one: about two-thirds of its people live in cities, of whom more than 60 per cent live in and around the six state capitals of Adelaide, Brisbane, Hobart, Melbourne, Perth, and Sydney, and less than 15 per cent in rural areas. Most of the population is concentrated along the eastern and southeastern coastlines with one-third in New South Wales and a further quarter in Victoria. Here, the climate is more equable, and, by British standards, blessed by long hours of sunshine, which enable Australians to enjoy the outdoors recreational activities in which they revel. Australia also has a unique and remarkable flora and fauna, including a bewitching and bewildering variety of birds, boasting some 800 species. The country has a wide range of scenery and, having in recent years become more environmentally conscious, has developed a growing number of National and State Parks.

The social and economic background

Australia, is, of course, by European standards a relatively young country, and in 1988 celebrates the bi-centenary of the first European settlement on the continent. In the two centuries that have followed and, especially since the end of the Second World War, it has become probably the most polyglot country in the world. Until then the great majority of its inhabitants were of Anglo-Celtic stock, coming in roughly equal numbers from the United Kingdom and Ireland. Thus, in a recent census, of those professing the Christian faith just over a quarter were Anglican and almost exactly the same number were Roman Catholic. Since 1945, however, some four million migrants have settled in Australia from more than 120 countries: in the 1950s and 1960s from Greece, Italy and Yugoslavia, in particular; and more recently from South-East Asia. The great majority of these immigrants are concentrated in specific parts of the major cities. As a consequence, a significant proportion of children in Australian schools come from non-English-speaking backgrounds: at the 1981 Census, for example, over 40 percent of the population was either born overseas or born in Australia with at least one overseas-born parent; and 21 per cent of the Australian population was of non-English speaking background. The original inhabitants of the continent, the Aboriginals, now constitute just over 1 per cent of the total population and about two-thirds of them live in cities and towns.

Given the geo-political realities of its situation, it is hardly surprising that since the war Australia has moved many of its cultural and political allegiances away from Western Europe to the Pacific basin. There is an inreasing awareness of its links with the other countries on the Pacific rim and a growing interest, as evidenced by frequent articles in newspapers and magazines, in economic and political developments in the region. In broad political terms, Australia is a federation with a Commonwealth Government, based at Canberra, the country's capital, and six state governments, in New South Wales, Victoria, Queensland, South Australia, Western Australia, and Tasmania respectively. In addition, the Northern Territory is similar to the states in that it is largely self-governing, while the Australian Capital Territory (ACT), the relatively small area comprising Canberra and the immediate countryside, is fully dependent on the Commonwealth Government.

Federation was reluctantly agreed to by the then independent colonies in 1901, when a constitution was approved which gave strictly limited powers to a relatively weak Federal Government, while the remaining, unspecified, powers stayed with the states. Since then, however, the power of the central government has increased slowly but inexorably, especially in the post-war period, at the expense of the state governments. Although national patriotism has grown, particularly in recent years, the great majority of Australians still feel a strong sense of state identity which expresses itself in inter-state rivalry, especially in sporting events, as well as in other ways.

During the past thirty years or so, the Australian economy has undergone considerable change and expansion. Before the last war it depended mainly on its agricultural products such as wool, meat and grain but, since about the 1960s, exports of non-farm primary products such as iron ore, bauxite and coal, especially to Japan, have also become very important. Moreover, during and particularly after the war the manufacturing sector grew rapidly, mainly in the heavy industries such as iron and steel, fertilisers, petroleum, heavy chemicals, and paper and plastics. Since then, Australia's manufacturing base has been broadened to include advanced technology, such as the manufacture of electronic devices. However, manufacturing is inevitably restricted by the limited size of the domestic market, as compared to Western Europe for example, by the wide geographical dispersion of industrial plants, and by Australia's distance from accessible markets. In this respect, as in so many others, Australia is beset by the 'tyranny' of distance. Nevertheless, during the 1950s and 1960s, the standard of living in Australia grew appreciably, so that its citizens enjoyed such a degree of affluence, spread relatively widely throughout the country, that Donald Horne coined the term, still widely used to describe it, 'The Lucky Country'. During much of the past twelve years, however, Australia, like most of the rest of the developed world, has been living through a major recession. The world-wide down-turn in trade drastically reduced demand for the products of which Australia is a leading producer, so that the export prices of coal, metals, wheat and wool, for example, have all been adversely affected. Manufacturing and construction has also been hard hit with the result that, as we shall see, the training of apprentices, for example, has been affected and youth unemployment has substantially increased. The trade unions are particularly powerful in the manual trades, and their attitudes to apprenticeship training have also been an important factor. Moreover, Australian manufacturing industry, like that in the United Kingdom, has also been profoundly affected by the strength of the Japanese economy.

On the other hand, in recent decades the tertiary or service sector of the economy has been growing in relative importance, until today it accounts for almost three-quarters of the total Australian employment. The major employer in this sector has been the retail and wholesale trade, but financial and business services, community services, recreation and tourism and, indeed, education, have all greatly increased. In many of these areas there are serious shortages of skilled personnel. Nevertheless, during the last fifteen years or so, youth unemployment has increasingly become a feature of Australian economic life. Traditionally, the majority of young Australians left school at 15 or 16 and entered full-time employment, many of the young men as apprentices. As a result of technological change and economic recession, the number of full-time jobs, and especially unskilled and semi-skilled jobs, began to decline, and unemployment began to grow. By April 1987 it had reached a level of over 8 per cent of the population as a whole, and was running at 20.5 per cent of teenagers and 10.9 per cent for 20– to 24–year-olds.[1] One of the major consequences has been the growing concern, as in the United Kingdom, to provide vocational education and training, which will both raise the skills of youngsters leaving school, and also keep them off the labour market until they acquire the kinds of skills likely to lead them to find a job. In Australia, as in the United Kingdom, in recent years the relationship between education and the labour market has become the subject of much consideration, resulting in several significant and influential reports, of which perhaps the most far-seeing is the 1985 Report of the Kirby Committee on Labour Market Programmes.

The educational background

As a product of Australia's federal system of government, the country has no fewer than eight distinct systems of education, one each in the six states, in the Northern Territory and in the Australian Capital Territory (ACT). As a result there are significant differences in provision and administration between the eight systems though, as is to be expected, they have a great deal in common. In the six states and the Northern Territory, the provision of education services is their own responsibility, while in the ACT and a few small external territories it is the responsibility of the Federal Government. In addition, the Commonwealth Government makes grants to the states for specific educational purposes.

School attendance is compulsory between the ages of 6 and 15 in all states except Tasmania, where the leaving age is 16. However, a substantial majority of children attend some form of pre-school education and, indeed, almost all complete at least ten years of schooling from 5 to 15. A full span of school is taken to be twelve years from 5 to 17, when youngsters can enter higher education, but only about 45 per cent complete the twelve years. Although, as in the United Kingdom, drop-out rates are related to cultural background and socieconomic status,[2] in recent years the percentage of those staying on in school has markedly increased. The school system is divided into primary schools which cater for youngsters up to the age of 12, and secondary schools which can be attended until the age of 17. The most common type of secondary school is the co-educational comprehensive school though, in some states, there are separate, specialist high schools concentrating on technical, agricultural or commerical subjects, or offering home economics. Victoria is unusual among the states in still having technical schools, though they are declining in number. The Victorian technical schools accommodate the majority of off-the-job apprenticeship training in the state and their facilities are adequate to meet the requirements of all but a few trades.

The great majority of Australian youngsters, some 78 per cent at primary level and about 72 per cent at secondary level, attend non-fee paying state schools or, as they are termed, 'government' schools. However, the private sector is of considerable importance in Australia, though its incidence and importance vary from state to state. The majority of private schools are run by the Roman Catholic church, mainly in systems organised on a state-wide basis and charging relatively low fees. Most other private schools are associated with other religious denominations, notably the Anglican Church, and they are often highly sought after and charge high fees. This last group of schools has been particularly influential in Australian public life as it has produced a disproportionate number of the leading members of the professions and the government services. The schools are more numerous in some states than others, being particularly important in Victoria for example, but they have all benefited until fairly recently from the fact that large sums of money have been made available from Commonwealth funds to all registered private schools, both rich and expensive private schools and poor parochial, Roman Catholic schools. Within the last few years, however, public funds have been directed more towards the needy state-wide Catholic parochial systems and away from the expensive single private schools.

Be that as it may, the secondary school system is followed, logically enough, by the tertiary sector of education, which in Australia denotes the whole-range of post-secondary education and very largely falls into three parts (see Figure 2.1): the Universities, the Colleges of Advanced Education, and the Colleges of Technical and Further Education (or TAFE, for short). There are a few exceptions to this simple, tripartite division: in Queensland, for example, there are Rural Training Schools and Senior Colleges which fall outside the precise definition of TAFE colleges. In broad terms, however, the British equivalents of the three major groups of institutions are the Universities; the Polytechnics and

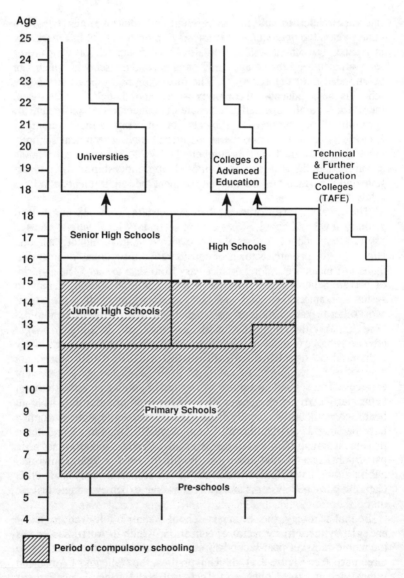

Figure 2.1 The educational system in Australia

Colleges/Institutes of Higher Education; and the Technical Colleges and Colleges of Further Education. As in the United Kingdom, vocational education and training at technician and craft level is very largely concentrated in the third group of institutions and it is with these that we shall be primarily concerned.

Although, to some extent, the lines of demarcation between the three types of post-secondary institutions are becoming blurred, in general terms higher education is largely restricted to the first two, that is the twenty Universities and forty-four Colleges of Advanced Education (or Institutes of Advanced Education/Technology as they are called in some states). However, for the purpose of disbursing federal funds, all three are covered by the Commonwealth Tertiary Education Commission (CTEC) which began life as the Tertiary Education Commission in 1977 by subsuming previously separate funding bodies for each of the three sectors, and assumed its new title in 1981.[3] It is subdivided into three subordinate Advisory Councils, one each for the Universities (UAC), Advanced Education (HEAC), and Technical and Further Education (TAFEAC). The essential difference, in financial terms, between the first two and the third, is that the universities and colleges derive their funds wholly from the Commonwealth Government through the CTEC, while the TAFE colleges derive their funds partly from the CTEC and partly from the states. In all, approximately one-quarter of the relevant age group enter some form of higher education institutions which, like the TAFE colleges, charge no tuition fees for non-'adult education' courses.

The provision of vocational education and training

In Australia, as in the United Kingdom, vocational education and training is provided by three main agencies: the public system of Technical and Further Education; private institutions offering vocational training; and industry itself. Australia is also like the United Kingdom, from which its system largely derives, in that the bulk of formal provision is made by the first agency, the public institutions of vocational education and training and, unlike Japan, Australian industry has traditionally relied upon them to provide the bulk of the training. It is upon these institutions, therefore, that this chapter will largely concentrate.

Technical and Further Education and its widely used acronym TAFE are relatively recent terms. Dating from 1974, the term 'Technical and Further Education' can be seen broadly to reflect the major activities within the sector, namely vocational and pre-vocational education, and what, in the United Kingdom, would be described as recreational and liberal Adult Education, although in Australia the term 'enrichment' is used as a synonym for 'liberal'. As in this country, however, there is a degree of overlap between the two. Although 'technical colleges' of one sort and another have long existed, and those offering programmes in mining or agriculture, for example, are among the most venerable of Australian educational institutions, it was not until the 1970s that the sector as a whole — broadly equivalent to Non-Advanced Further Education (NAFE) in the United Kingdom — began to acquire a national identity and was recognised by the Commonwealth Government as an important national resource.[4]

Prior to 1974, technical education came to be regarded as the 'poor relation', compared to the other two sectors of post-school education, namely the Universities and the Colleges of Advanced Education (CAEs), into which, by the early 1970s, the Commonwealth Government was pumping increasingly large sums of money. As a result, TAFE inevitably suffered from an inferiority complex which, even in today's much improved circumstances, still lingers in places. However, in 1973 the Commonwealth Government, recognising the importance of technical education to the economic well-being of the nation, established a Committee under the chairmanship of a distinguished lawyer, Meyer Kangan, to review the needs of TAFE and to make recommendations for its future development. The Kangan Report,[5] published in 1974, marks a watershed in the fortunes of TAFE; the main burden of its message was that in the last part of the twentieth century TAFE must be seen as an alternative, one neither inferior nor superior, to the other two streams of post-secondary education. The wisdom of this message was acknowledged by the Commonwealth Government which provided substantial funds, both capital and recurrent, in addition to those being provided by the state governments, in order to raise the profile of TAFE as the major povider of basic vocational training in Australia.

Major administrative changes also followed in the wake of the Kangan Report including the establishment of the first Commonwealth TAFE Commission, the vehicle by which Commonwealth funds for TAFE would be directed to the states. In 1977, as we have seen, the Tertiary Education Commission (TEC) was set up, later to become the CTEC, to cover all three sectors of post-secondary education, and the TAFE Committee was subsumed into it as one of three subordinate Councils for Universities, Colleges of Advanced Education and TAFE respectively.

Since then, student participation in TAFE has grown considerably, so that by the mid-1980s there were more than one million students in about 230 institutions in the TAFE sector, making it by far the largest part of tertiary education. As many of the institutions cater for a population spread over large geographical areas, they operate on multi-sites and, in all, the 230 institutions operate in about 1,000 different locations. Many of the colleges are either relatively new, having been built in the post-Kangan era, or have been enlarged and modernised. On the whole they are well-equipped and furnished and, in appearance, broadly similar to British colleges of futher education. However, the geographical distribution of the Australian population poses TAFE with special difficulties. In New South Wales, for example, no fewer than 58 per cent of the state's population live in Sydney, with the remaining 42 per cent widely dispersed among country centres. Providing a sufficiently broad range of vocational courses in country areas where student numbers are small and thinly scattered, and where accommodation and facilities are often scarce and costly is a continuing problem.[6] Across the state enrolments run at over 350,000 a year — the largest number in any state — attending well over a thousand courses offered in a hundred or so colleges with about 200 small teaching centres in outlying settlements. In the more remote areas, mobile instructional units, including five railway and three road units equipped for use as workshops and training schools, are deployed. In addition, there is an External Studies College of TAFE, based in Sydney, through which some 30,000 students receive correspondence courses with tutorial and other support from local colleges. In all these respects, and allowing for differences of scale, New South Wales is typical of the other states.

As TAFE is offered and organised on a state basis, there are eight systems which, although they have a great deal in common, differ in detail and in the ways they are organised: each is the product of such factors as size, history, legislation, geographical considerations, and prevailing political ideologies.[7] In some states, such as New South Wales and Victoria, varying degrees of regional organisation and devolution have been adopted. Victoria has probably gone furthest along these lines by setting-up in 1983 its own TAFE Board as an independent authority separate from the State Education Department, and by establishing Regional TAFE Boards to which many responsibilities are devolved. In other states, however, notably Queensland, a higher level of centralised control is maintained, although in recent years there has been some devolution of responsibilities to the colleges:[8] one by-product of this centralisation is the tension which exists between the up-country TAFE colleges and the state capital, Brisbane, with some of the former believing that neither are their problems fully understood, nor their best interests served, by the high level of centralised power. The primary educational and financial responsibility for the TAFE sector rests with the state and Northern Territory governments but, as we have seen, since the mid-1970s the Commonwealth Government has been injecting substantial funds into the state systems. These contributions are mainly in the area of capital works such as building and equipment but, in addition, considerable sums of money are earmarked for specific purposes such as staff development, curriculum development, improved management systems, and provisions for special groups such as unemployed young people, migrants, handicapped people, and the educationally disadvantaged. In all, the Commonwealth Government contributes about

35 per cent of all the money spent on TAFE, with the majority of it coming through the CTEC. In addition, however, substantial sums flow from what was the Department of Employment and Industrial Relations (DEIR) in Canberra and is now the Department of Employment, Education and Training, constituting about one-third of the Commonwealth's total contribution, for what it calls 'labour market programmes'. These include recent initiatives such as the Australian Traineeship System (ATS) for young school-leavers (the equivalent of the British Youth Training Scheme), the Youth Training Programme, to provide short-term vocational opportunities for unemployed young people, and the Adult Training Programme to enhance the vocational training and retraining of adults.

The functions and purposes of Australian TAFE are, of course, manifold, and have grown in recent years in response to the increasing complexity of Australian society, and such factors as youth unemployment and the need to make provision for migrants and refugees. As in the United Kingdom, the TAFE colleges offer a broad range of courses which until recently were officially categorised into six 'Streams of Study' (Table 2.1). As will be seen, in 1984 there were just over 1,300,000 TAFE students, of whom just over half were enrolled in vocational courses which, broadly speaking, embraced the first four streams. Preparatory courses, which denote general education up to the standards required for entrance into institutions of higher education, enrolled over 16 per cent; and almost one-third of TAFE students were undertaking adult education 'enrichment' courses catering for recreational and general interests. By comparison with the United Kingdom, the proportion of students on vocational courses in TAFE is much higher, reflecting in part its heavy commitment to apprenticeship training. Moreover, Australia has not experienced the steep decline in apprenticeships which the United Kingdom has undergone in the past decade. The age range of Australian TAFE is, of course, very large and, indeed, persons aged 25 and over represent a clear majority of the total student population. However, although young people aged 16 to 20 are in the minority, as many of them are attending courses on a full-time or day-release basis, they take up a disproportionate amount of teaching resources. The dramatic increase in TAFE enrolments in recent years by youngsters has meant that, although TAFE tries to impose few if any restrictions of access on its student population, pressure for places has been so strong that some institutions in some states have had to be selective in their intakes. Throughout Australia, the number of youngsters staying on in school after the statutory leaving age has grown, assisted in part by joint programmes with TAFE, and by the acceptance of some school courses for credit transfer into TAFE programmes. As a consequence, the enrolment of teenagers in TAFE courses is outstripping the relative decline in their proportion of the total population.

Table 2.1 Australian TAFE students by stream of study, 1984

Stream of study	Student numbers ('000)	%
Professional	3.3	0.3
Para-professional	245.2	18.8
Trade	147.2	11.3
Other skilled	268.9	20.7
Preparatory	213.9	16.4
Adult Education	423.1	32.5
Total	1,301.6*	100

(Source: Department of Employment and Industrial Relations, Canberra)
*This total is in excess of the total number of students enrolled on TAFE courses as some students are enrolled in more than one stream of study.

As Table 2.2 shows, the total size of the Australian 16 to 20 age-group in 1986 was just over 1,300,000. Of these, over one-third were attending full-time courses of education, mainly in schools; almost one-half were in full-time employment, a quarter of them undertaking apprenticeships; and the remainder were either unemployed or in none of the above groups. As in the United Kingdom, the number of young people in full-time employment has declined markedly in the past decade, while the proportion of unemployed youngsters has sharply increased, and by 1987 had reached approximately one-fifth of the total work force, that is those not in full-time education.

As in the United Kingdom, the traditional method of vocational training for youngsters leaving school and entering employment has been by *apprenticeship*. Indeed, the system was imported from the United Kingdom a century or more ago, and remains very much intact. Throughout the period of its existence it has always played an important part in what in Australia is called 'trade training', that is, training at craft level, and annually some 45,000 young people leave school to enter apprenticeships. As part of their apprenticeship programme they are required to attend off-the-job training courses in TAFE colleges, usually on a day or block-release basis. However, the precise requirements vary from state to state: for example, the length of release necessary to complete one stage of a programme varies from 30 days in Tasmania and Western Australia to 40 days in Victoria and the Northern Territory.

In recent years the annual intake of apprentices has varied somewhat. Due to the economic recession there was a sharp reduction in 1982–3 and, to a lesser extent, in 1983–4, after which the numbers picked up and they are currently running at between 45,000 and 50,000 a year.

Table 2.2 Australia: the 16–19 age group, 1986

	('000)	%
Full-time students		
Schools	314.9	
TAFE	52.0	
Higher education	115.0	
	481.9	36.8
Full-time employment		
Apprenticeships	99.6	
Traineeships	1.1	
Other	484.6	
	585.3	44.4
Unemployed	151.4	11.4
Other		
Neither full-time students,		
nor in the full-time		
labour force)	98.4	7.4
Totals	1,317.0	100.0

(Source: *Skills For Australia*, Australian Government Publishing Service, Canberra, 1987, p. 41)

These numbers are such that the system is comparable in volume to the university and college of advanced education systems combined.[9] In its broad-ranging review of Australia's training system, *Skills for Australia*, issued in 1987, the Commonwealth Government estimates that an average annual intake of some 45,000 apprentices is required to meet the long-term needs of the economy, and maintain an adequate level and quality of trade skills. Of the present pool of apprentices undergoing trade training, the great majority are male: in South Australia, for example, in 1984–5 only about 12 per cent were female and, if hairdressers were excluded, this figure fell to 4 per cent. There has been a slow increase of female participation in the trades traditionally dominated by men, but it remains very slow despite initiatives both by the Commonwealth Government and also by state governments to foster it.

Although statuory responsibility for the administration of apprenticeships rests with the states and territories, the Commonwealth Government has for many years provided substantial financial support, principally through its Commonwealth Rebate for Apprentice Full-time Training (CRAFT) scheme, which was introduced in 1977. As a consequence of its introduction, the average annual level of intake to apprenticeships in the past decade has risen from about 34,000 to over 45,000.

As the training arrangements for apprentices vary from state to state, and as the training practices of employers vary even more, so the common core of skills provided by off-the-job training in the TAFE colleges is very important in ensuring that apprentices achieve minimum levels of skill. Following the recommendations made in the 1985 Kirby Report, the DEIR co-ordinated national moves to improve the apprenticeship training system, and to achieve consistency across the states. Accordingly, TAFE systems have been called upon to devise and implement national common core curricula, a measure accepted by the state directors of TAFE, and to review curricula regularly to ensure they meet the changing needs of industry. One suggested model is that, in their earlier stages, curricula should be broadly-based in respect of related trades, to be followed by specialised electives or modules. While much of the teaching of apprenticeships is traditional and straightforward, there is scope for individual colleges and, indeed, individuals within colleges, to introduce original methods of instruction. One such example is the system of 'self-paced learning' based on a modular instruction programme at which the student learns at his or her own rate, used very successfully by Richmond College of TAFE, in Melbourne, Victoria, for apprentices in the motor-vehicle trade.

Associated with apprentice training, an important and interesting development in recent years has been the substantial increase in the number of school-leavers undertaking trade-based pre-employment (TBPE) courses in TAFE colleges. The major subject areas are those available in the colleges: in Queensland, for example, they comprise engineering and construction, graphic arts, tourism and catering, business studies, horticulture, and the marine industry. The courses, which grant exemption from some part of the subsequent apprenticeship, have come to be accepted by employers, unions and the young people themselves, as alternatives to direct entry to apprenticeship, with the result that TAFE enrolments in these courses rose from a few hundred in 1973 to about 10,000 in 1985. In the last few years the Commonwealth Government has helped the expansion of TBPE training in TAFE colleges by funding additional course places, up to a total of 2,000 in 1988, including 500 places to assist young women. However, it has not been uncritical of TBPE training in the colleges, arguing that, given its complementary nature to that of apprentice training, it should develop more flexibility in deploying resources between the two, and that it should improve the standard of practical training provided by making greater use of training facilities in industry, particularly the off-the-job training centres which some of the larger firms have established in order to provide structured training programmes for their apprentices.[10]

The nationwide arrangement of apprenticeship systems with its off-the-job training in TAFE colleges has, by current practices in the United Kingdom, something of an old-fashioned, if sturdy and comforting, appearance. To an extent this is dictated by Australian circumstances. An apprentice in the printing trade, for example, may find himself working in a small, remote countrytown where, by the standards of Sydney or Brisbane, the equipment is old-fashioned and antiquated, and his training must take this into account. On the other hand, some trenchant critics of the apprenticeship system maintain that substantial parts of it are inefficient and expensive to run. Moreover, as it is concentrated in a limited number of traditional, and to a degree declining industries, such as metal-working and building, it is not meeting the contemporary needs of society. Indeed, three-quarters of apprenticeships are to be found in three major industrial areas: manufacturing with 31 per cent, construction with 25 per cent, and the wholesale and retail trades with 18 per cent.

Apprenticeship training is, indeed, expensive and in 1985 it was estimated to cost the public purse alone between 6,600 and 14,500 Australian dollars per apprentice for the indenture period. (In July 1987, for example, the pound sterling was worth approximately 2.3 Australian dollars.) For these reasons, Professor Peter Karmel, a distinguished educationist and a former chairman of the CTEC, has advocated a training scheme which would overcome some of the limitations of the present arrangements, such as the bias against young women and its restriction to certain industries. The present arrangements have also been criticised by Peter Kirby, the chairman of the Committee of Inquiry into Labour Market Programmes, on the grounds that, for all their virtues, they have obstructed the development of systems for retraining older people, a growing contemporary need.

There now seems to be a broad measure of agreement that the apprenticeship system needs to be made more flexible and more responsible to the needs of industry and to advances in technology. As in the United Kingdom, there is a growing awareness that skills training must become more broadly-based and multi-skilled in character and, in the words of a recent Commonwealth Government publication, must 'be moved from a time-serving to a competency basis, and become a significant component in a ladder of continuous skills development.'[11] As a result, the Commonwealth Government has undertaken a review of its apprenticeship support programmes and, from 1 January 1988, will be introducing changes into its CRAFT scheme and other programmes of financial support, with a view to maintaining the incentive for employers to continue to recruit sufficient numbers of apprentices, and to emphasise the need to provide training programmes which produce skilled workers and ensure a high level of completion.

With the increasing scale of unemployment among young people, the Commonwealth Government, like governments in the United States and the United Kingdom, has introduced training programmes to give them marketable skills and to take them off the labour market. Since 1983, when the Labour Government led by Robert Hawke came into power at Canberra, no fewer than five significant initiatives have been introduced: the *Participation and Equity Programme* (PEP), the *Australian Traineeship System*, the *Adult Training Programme*, and, most recently, the *Youth Training Programme*, and the *Skills Training Programme*.

The *Participation and Equity Programme* (PEP) has had only a short life, being first introduced in 1984, and then abolished on 1 January, 1988, to be replaced by other programmes. Nevertheless, during that time it had a considerable impact on the TAFE colleges. Prior to 1984 a programme to improve the employment prospects of young people in education was already in existence, namely, the School to Work Transition Programme, and PEP built on this earlier scheme by using its materials, courses and staff, sometimes with little adaptation. The major difference between them, however, was that PEP, in theory at least, concentrated on reducing the supply of labour by retaining youngsters in the education system, rather than improving the quality of the supply of youth labour. PEP was aimed at young people aged between 15 and 24, and its main purpose was to offer them a broad experience of education and training which would provide a foundation for both their working and non-working lives.[12] The programme also placed a strong emphasis on 'equity' by requiring the development of courses from which the less-advantaged groups in the community could benefit.[13] The potential target population was very large, as the CTEC estimated that some 340,000 young people throughout Australia were unemployed or had dropped out of both education and the labour market. PEP courses were provided both by TAFE and by the secondary schools, and in its first year, 1984, just over 70 million Australian dollars were made available for this purpose by the Commonwealth Government, of which over a third went to TAFE, which was enjoined to facilitate 'equity' by improving the employability and self-confidence of disadvantaged young people. The division of responsibility for providing PEP courses between secondary schools and TAFE colleges has had variable results: in some cases the two sectors have co-operated well, in others they have vied for supremacy. Moreover, the programme has, inevitably perhaps, been determined by two, sometimes competing, philosophies. The TAFE colleges and the DEIR have tended to take a more 'instrumental' view and be mainly concerned with producing trained personnel, while the Commonwealth Schools Commission and the Department of Education have concentrated on providing a more general education. Initially, PEP courses in the TAFE colleges concentrated on providing basic skills, but the trainees themselves wanted courses with a specific vocational orientation as they were more likely to provide them with marketable skills. As a result, PEP courses with a strong vocational orientation became the norm, and eventually comprised 70 per cent of the total. Indeed, TAFE colleges and secondary schools were often finding difficulty in filling all the places on the basic skills courses. Moreover, although the initial focus of the PEP programme was to provide early school-leavers with a bridge from school to work, it changed later and concentrated on providing training programmes for older youth who lacked the skills to find a job. As a consequence, 70 per cent of PEP trainees were 18 years of age or older.

In 1985 approximately 18,000 young people participated in PEP-funded courses in TAFE colleges; the courses themselves were financed by the CTEC and, in addition, most trainees received what used to be called a 'Transition Allowance', or maintenance grant, from the Department of Employment and Industrial Relations. The Transition Allowance was then subsumed into an age-related allowance system which applies to all government-funded normal training programmes. However, with the introduction of the Australian Traineeship system and the Adult Training Programme, government funds for PEP were drastically cut, with the result that in its last year of operation, 1987, only about 9,000 trainees were attending PEP courses in TAFE colleges. When PEP was abolished at the beginning of 1988 it was replaced by provision in the Adult Training Programme (ATP) and by two new programmes, the Youth Training Programme and the Skills Training Programme, each of which will be described later in the chapter.

It was in 1985 that the Hawke national government announced a major new initiative as part of 'a national youth strategy' to deal especially with youth unemployment, named the *Australian Traineeship System*(ATS). Youth unemployment had grown considerably over the previous decade, and by August 1984 the unemployment rate among 15–to–19-year-olds seeking full-time work had grown to about 24 per cent, though as we have seen it subsequently declined somewhat, to 20.5 per cent in April 1987. The ATS initiative stemmed from the recommendations of the 1985 Kirby Report on Labour Market Programmes which advocated a broadly -based traineeship system consisting of formal off-the-job education and training complemented by work in a related occupation. The traineeships, to be provided initially for 16–to–17-year-old school-leavers, should be a minimum of one year's duration with at least thirteen weeks off-the-job training covering broad-based skills relating to 'families of occupations'. Initially, therefore, ATS was closely modelled on the British Youth Training Scheme, but, as it has developed, it has moved away from it in some respects and, compared to the Kirby Report model, it has placed more emphasis on training and less on continuing education. The initial expectations for ATS were undoubtedly over-ambitious: in 1985, for example, the government was officially aiming for a target of 10,000 traineeships in 1986, to rise to an annual intake of at least 75,000 by 1988–9.[14] As we shall see, the scale of the scheme has turned out to be very much smaller. In outline, the system required each trainee to spend one-quarter of his traineeship year in off-the-job training, the bulk of which was to be provided by the TAFE colleges. Clearly, the implications of ATS for the Australian TAFE colleges, like that of YTS for its British counterparts, are very considerable.

The first ATS trainees began their programmes in 1986 and, by the end of August 1987, 9,154 of them had places on the scheme and 11,416 places had been created or agreed with industry. Of these, about 60 per cent were in the public sector, in branches of the Commonwealth and state governments, and the other 40 per cent in the private sector, mainly in banking, retail chain stores, advertising agencies and tourism and hospitality. Approximately two-thirds of the traineeships were held by females and one-third by males, and two-thirds of them were aged 16 or 17. Fifteen per cent of all places are available to the disadvantaged, including Aboriginals and the handicapped, and a form of bridging course is provided for them. As might be supposed, their geographical spread is very largely confined to the cities and the larger towns and, indeed, some 80 per cent of all traineeships are available in the capital cities.

In the rush to get the scheme off the ground, the existing infrastructure was used, namely the seven State Training (Labour Market) Authorities responsible for overseeing apprenticeships, in which the Commonwealth and state governments, industry, the unions and the TAFE colleges all have members. Curricula, or training packages, are designed by Industry Working Groups, in which the same interests are represented. Group Training Schemes have been established to enable smaller employers who do not normally have the capacity to take on trainees for the whole year to take part in the scheme and also to provide the maximum opportunities for rural areas.

As with the British Youth Training Scheme, the provision of high-quality training packages has inevitably proved difficult. In the case of the on-the-job training element, there has been some union opposition to some of the proposals, partly because of fears that employers would use the trainees as cheap labour, and many employers are not in a position to offer the full training experience required. In the past few years, however, a substantial measure of agreement has been reached and, by August 1987, 143 industrial agreements involving 36 trades unions had been accomplished. Another requirement of an effective programme is that the progress of trainees be effectively monitored, and guidelines for employers have been devised. Although ATS has not been going long enough properly to assess the effectiveness of the monitoring process, it would appear to be working reasonably well.[15]

The off-the-job element takes place mainly in the TAFE colleges, and a core curriculum devised by one state TAFE system has since been adopted nationally by the colleges. In broad terms, trainees attend TAFE colleges for about 400 hours over the 36-week teaching year, that is, for between one-and-a-half and two days a week over that period. Initially, both absenteeism and drop-out rates were high on these courses, but there seems to have been some improvement during the last year or two. Certificates are now awarded to trainees on completion of the programme and all states and territories have now agreed on a common approach which should ensure the integrity of the certificate. The scope of the scheme is also gradually widening and traineeships are currently being developed in metal fabrication, printing, plastics and community services, and will be extended to manufacturing, where hitherto they have not been regarded as compatible with apprenticeships. The Commonwealth Government is according a high priority to ATS with a view to ensuring that it become a major means of entry into the labour market for young people. Accordingly, it made substantial additional funds available in its 1987 Budget in order to provide places for some 20,000 young Australians in the year 1987-8.

Visitors from the United Kingdom examining the progress of ATS must inevitably experience a strong feeling of *déjà-vu*, as they see it encountering many of the same problems met by YTS. It must also be said that ATS does not yet appear to have impinged much on the consciousness of Australian society, to whom it remains largely an unknown quantity. Yet, as with YTS, ATS would seem to be a more or less permanent feature of the Australian training system and, as its numbers grow, so its influence on the TAFE system will increase. As in the United Kingdom it is introducing into the colleges a 'new' clientele, many of whom have been alienated from education while at school and are not in the colleges because they wish to be there. The enormous challenge for TAFE throughout Australia is for the colleges to offer programmes which will both appeal to these youngsters and also promote their education and training. The requirements are for innovative forms of education and training and for close liaison with industry and State Training Authorities to ensure, among other things, that off-the-job training in the colleges relates to, and complements, on-the-job training in industry.

The third Commonwealth Government initiative in the training field is its *Adult Training Programme* (ATP). Introduced following the recommendation of the Kirby Report which identified the training and retraining needs of adults as those most neglected by existing schemes, ATP, which replaced a number of existing programmes, started on 1 January, 1986. Its principal aim is to enable adults who have been unemployed for six months or longer, and who lack the skills to find jobs or have been declared redundant (or 'retrenched' in the Australian vernacular), to undertake suitable training courses. These courses, many of which are provided by the TAFE colleges, are of varying duration and the adults attending them obtain financial assistance from the Commonwealth Government. There is, of course, nothing particularly new about such courses and TAFE colleges had already been providing retraining courses, for example, for workers displaced from the steel industry. However, lack of financial and other resources had limited their extent and the pumping-in of Commonwealth funds for this purpose has enabled them to be substantially increased. By the end of its first year ATP had assisted about 8,700 adults, and in May 1987 the Commonwealth Government announced that it would be providing a significant increase in funding to provide training courses for an estimated 13,000 adults. Among the specific groups to be provided for are migrants with overseas professional qualifications seeking to obtain recognition of these qualifications in Australia, by means of appropriate bridging and retraining courses, and single parents and women, returning to the labour market after significant periods of absence. A number of TAFE colleges have tailored their existing courses to meet the particular requirements of these two groups of trainees.

During 1987, the Commonwealth Government introduced what it described as a major new training initiative in the form of the *Youth Training Programme*, which is designed to provide a range of short-term vocational training opportunities for unemployed young people. The scheme replaces those parts of PEP and the Adult Training Programme aimed at 15-to-20-year-olds and combines them into a single programme which makes use of TAFE off-the-job courses to complement specifically arranged training packages. The Youth Training Programme is also intended to expand significantly the training opportunities available to disadvantaged young people. In all, about 13,000 young people were expected to be assisted under the Youth Training Programme in 1987–8, and a further expansion is planned for 1988–9.

Finally, the Commonwealth Government provided limited funds in 1987–8 for a new *Skills Training Programme* which is designed to develop innovative training projects, including Skills Centres, and to give continuing support to the national network of Industry Training Committees (see p. 63). According to the Commonwealth Government, the money will be used 'carefully and selectively' where the training provided falls outside the traditional province of the TAFE system or where the capacity of TAFE is limited or at a premium, and where the skills to be provided 'are of strategic significance in terms of industry restructuring and international competitiveness'.[16]

These various initiatives constitute a gradually accelerating policy by the Hawke Commonwealth Government since it came into office in 1983, to ensure that Australia's system of education and training respond to what it perceives to be the country's needs for skilled personnel. As we have seen, following its re-election for its third term of office in July 1987, a new 'super-ministry', the federal Department of Employment, Education and Training (DEET) was established in order to give a higher priority to, and co-ordinate, the provision of 'education and skills development'. Among the goals the new ministry has set itself are, to increase the national training capacity, improve the quality and flexibility of the training systems, raise the level of private sector investment in training, improve the employment and training opportunities available to the unemployed and disadvantaged, and reduce the high level of occupational segregation by sex in the labour market. All these are desirable goals, but how effectively and quickly they will be achieved remain to be seen, and some of them, like sexual occupational segregation, are very intractable problems.

In the meantime, recognising the key role that the TAFE system will play in all this, the DEET is restructuring its TAFE funding from 1 January 1988. The purposes of this restructuring are, in its own inelegant words (embodying a split infinitive), 'to better reflect national priorities and skills formation objectives, and to encourage greater industry participation'. In practice, the DEET will try to ensure that TAFE funds are spent 'in accordance with national priorities and in direct relationship to the government's broader economic and labour market objectives'. In addition, the TAFE system will be required to effect improvements in staff productivity and to introduce administrative arrangements to retain and increase revenues from entrepreneurial effort. Thus Federal Government policy, couched in very similar words, bears a strong and significant resemblance to measures introduced by the British Government through the agency of the Manpower Services Commission, not least the handing-over to the MSC of control of a proportion of the funds allocated to Work-Related Non-Advanced Further Education.

Among the groups of people identified by the Commonwealth and states governments in need of special help, particularly from the TAFE system, are the migrants and refugees who have come into Australia in recent years, and the country's oldest inhabitants, the Aboriginals, and the Torres Strait Islanders who live in the scattered islands between the northernmost tip of Queensland and New Guinea. Australia has for many years relied on a range of specific skills brought in with them by overseas workers. However, with growing unemployment in recent years, government policy has been in the somewhat awkward prose of the DEIR, 'to restrict skilled immigration in order to generate benefits to the economy without adversely affecting unemployed people, by ensuring that priority in employment is given to Australian residents'. Nevertheless, as we have seen, the past decade or so has witnessed a considerable influx into the country of non-English-speaking migrants and refugees, principally from South-East Asia who, together with their children, are in need of special help from the education and training system. Many of these migrants, and especially the refugees, do not bring into Australia the sorts of skills needed by the economy and are in need of the type of vocational training which the TAFE colleges can supply. In the great majority of cases they also lack the command of English required to perform effectively at work. For these, and other reasons, the unemployment rate for persons born outside Australia was 8.8 per cent in July 1987 compared with 7.5 per cent for those born in Australia, although there were clear differences between migrant groups of different ethnic backgrounds and periods of residence.

To a limited extent, TAFE colleges have for some years provided specific courses for migrants and their children, who, of course, also have access to the courses which they provide for the general public. However, there is some evidence to suggest that the migrant community in Australia is proportionally under-represented in the TAFE sector, while by contrast it avails itself much more readily of post-compulsory education in the secondary schools and institutions of higher education.[17] Two reasons for this may be that in the secondary schools they are concentrating upon improving their mastery of English; and because they face difficulties in gaining entry in certain trades, and so are deterred from taking relevant TAFE courses. However, in 1983 the Commonwealth Government transferred funds from the Department of Immigration and Ethnic Affairs to the CTEC and so into the TAFE systems, so that they could provide specific courses for adult migrants. These courses have two main aims: to increase the English proficiency of the migrants so that they can then enter training courses in TAFE or other post-secondary institutions; and to help migrants, who may already have skills, to develop an adequate command of English for occupational purposes. In addition, TAFE has also received specific funds to develop course curricula and materials, and to provide for staff development. Inevitably, this transfer of funds to TAFE aroused opposition from other quarters and, in any case, the funds have been rather limited. In the upshot, the reactions of the state TAFE departments have varied from the enthusiastic to the sluggardly. However, during the past few years some limited progress appears to have been made and, in New South Wales, for example, programmes have been operating within a general policy of multiculturalism, which is overseen by a special Multicultural Education Unit: among the courses provided are bridging courses for overseas-trained students in a range of occupations leading to enrolment in appropriate TAFE programmes; introductory courses aimed at specific vocational areas such as accounting; and pre-vocational courses designed to prepare students for selective test to enter various fields of employment. However, a major inhibiting factor in the more widespread development of such courses is that CTEC funds are only provided on an annual basis so that long-term planning is difficult. In addition, there has been a lack of support materials and there is insufficient information about the migrant population and their specific needs. Nevertheless, as we have seen, the TAFE colleges have in the past four years become more concerned with making provision for the migrant population, a concern which, if anything, is likely to grow in the foreseeable future.[18]

A subject of particular concern to the Commonwealth and state governments alike is to make suitable and sufficient provision of vocational training opportunities in TAFE for Aboriginals and Torres Strait Islanders. This population today numbers about 160,000; as we have seen, about two-thirds live in the cities and have adopted an urban lifestyle but, in addition, many live in the northern parts of the country or in the rural centres. Their social and economic conditions remain well below the standards of the average Australian, and although the Commonwealth Government has in recent years made some attempts to help them to regain control over their own lives, as indeed they wish to do, these attempts have not been notably successful. Aboriginals, lamentably, have an appallingly low rate of participation in post-secondary education and training and this, together with discrimination by employers and the down-turn in the Australian economy, has resulted in a high rate of Aboriginal unemployment, which is at least five times higher than the national unemployment rate. In response to this situation, the Federal Government initiated a National Employment Strategy for Aboriginals (NESA) designed to help them to obtain employment and training opportunities, including the provision of suitable courses in TAFE colleges. A few years ago, the Federal Government also commissioned a Committee of inquiry into Aboriginal Employment and Training Programmes. Its report, known as the Miller Report after its chairman, was published in August 1985 and drew attention to the fact that a good deal of money is made available by both Commonwealth and state governments for courses for Aboriginals in TAFE colleges which, however, are very largely recreational in nature. If effective vocational courses are to be provided, then special attention will have to be paid to the diverse and dispersed nature of Aboriginal needs. Moreover, at Commonwealth level, a number of departments of state, including Education, Employment and Training, and Aboriginal Affairs, are involved in promoting post-school education and vocational training for Aboriginals, a multiplication of bureaucratic working which, as the Miller Report points out, does not make for efficiency. However, it remains to be seen how far the recommendations of the Miller Report will be implemented.

In the meantime, individual states are making considerable efforts to meet the needs of the Aboriginal communities living within their borders. In Queensland, for example, where in addition to Aboriginals there are groups of Torres Strait Islanders, living in the scattered group of islands to the north of the mainland in not dissimilar social and economic circumstances, special courses are provided in some of the TAFE colleges to meet their particular needs and to enable them to enter regular TAFE courses. Where possible, the skills of indigenous counsellors, instructors, and teachers, are used, and indigenous field officers are based in most of the colleges. In New South Wales there is a widespread provision of mobile facilities in outback areas, and during the last few years special emphasis has been given to providing community-based vocational training programmes for the Aboriginal community, especially in the construction trades and in farm management and practice. However, the Aboriginal and Torres Strait Islanders in Australia are not infrequently treated as strangers in their own country. While attitudes towards them have changed for the better, much still needs to be done, and the TAFE colleges have a crucial role to play in providing appropriate vocational programmes.

As a result of social, economic and demographic changes similar to those which have occurred in the United Kingdom, there has been a dramatic increase in the last decade or two in the number of women employed in the Australian economy: in the 1970s alone their numbers increased by about 500,000, or just over 28 per cent.[19] Most of the increase has occurred in part-time employment and in technical and clerical occupations related to service industries such as tourism and recreation. This is reflected in the vocational courses which they undertake in TAFE colleges which, by and large, are restricted to the 'traditional' women's courses such as secretarial training. What is termed 'gender segregation' remains a prominent feature of Australian employment and is likely to change relatively slowly. As Ford points out, the culture of trade is 'overwhelmingly male chauvinist',[20] which contributes greatly to the notoriously low percentage of female tradespeople in Australia, compared to some other technological societies. However, the TAFE colleges have been playing a part in helping women and girls to enter occupational areas which have in the past been restricted to or dominated by men, by offering what are called 'affirmative action' programmes. In addition, many colleges provide bridging courses designed to acquaint women with the range of occupational and educational opportunities available to them; and remedial courses in such areas as literacy, numeracy and technical expertise, designed to overcome the effects of inappropriate or inadequate education and training. Although the take-up of these courses is relatively limited, it seems likely to expand in the foreseeable future. This expansion would undoubtedly be helped if, as suggested by Ford,[21] residential and child-care facilities were provided at key TAFE colleges. Although this provision is made more necessary by the increase in single-parent families and by the need of many women returning to the work force to update or upgrade their skills in order to obtain employment, Australia's straitened economic circumstances make it highly unlikely that additional money will be forthcoming for this purpose in the immediate future.

The widely dispersed nature of a high proportion of Australia's population has necessarily led over the years to the development of a well-established network of Distance Education, including many vocational programmes. These assume a variety of names in different states such as 'Outreach Programs', 'External Studies', and 'Technical Extension'. Typically, however, they are based on a central college: in New South Wales, for example, it is the External Studies College of TAFE in Sydney; in Queensland, the Technical Correspondence School in Brisbane; and, in Western Australia, the External Studies College in Perth. These colleges offer a very wide range of vocational programmes based primarily on correspondence courses. In addition, local TAFE colleges provide back-up in the form of tutorial help, sending tutors out to classes in private homes, community centres, church halls and other suitable locations, and also offer practical sessions, and learning resources. In Queensland, for example, no fewer than 400 individual vocational programmes are annually available in a wide range of subjects from the servicing of air-conditioning equipment, through electrical engineering, to the raising and management of sheep. Although the specific courses on offer and the way they are organised vary somewhat from state to state, they have certain features in common. By and large they offer open access with minimal entry qualifications; tuition is almost all free; it is possible to enter many courses at almost any time of the year; the pace at which students study is flexible, typically anything from six months to two years; the courses are structured so that students can choose particular elements which they feel they need, thereby enabling them to some extent to direct their own education; and efforts are made to ensure that projects and assignments are regularly assessed so that students have continuous feedback.[22]

On the other hand, distance education of this kind suffers from a number of intrinsic and traditional problems. One of the major ones is the lack of money which inhibits the introduction of new electronic technological equipment which could improve the system and which makes it difficult to evaluate properly existing courses and to introduce new, innovative ones. It is difficult, too, to find first-class teaching and support staff, who often have to stretch their expertise thinly over a large number of subjects and, for geographical and other reasons, there are often long delays in marking and returning assignments and projects. Most worrying of all, however, is the high drop-out rate among enrolled students which in Queensland, for example, runs at over 50 per cent in some courses. A similar situation obtains in Western Australia where in 1984 the Technical Extension Service received 16,000 enrolment forms from intending students, with the expectation that at least one-third of them would never even submit an assignment, though some of them have obtained all they required from the instructional material without wanting tuition.[23] Over the years 41 per cent of enrolments in the Western Australian Extension Service have been 'non-starters', a considerable waste of limited and expensive resources. Some idea of the extent of external studies in that particular state can be gauged from the fact that, in 1984, over 27,000 students enrolled in over 500 subjects, though some students applied for more than one subject at a time, taught by a teaching staff of 135 and a support staff of 78.

The reasons for the high drop-out rate, and for the substantial number of 'non-starters', common throughout the state systems, are manifold. There is often inadequate counselling before a student enrols on a course, he may lack personal support during his programme, and he may experience long delays in receiving feedback from his tutor. The courses are sometimes inadequately advertised, the student may have false expectations of them and, paradoxically, the very fact that they are free may cause them to be undervalued. The need to overcome these problems has led a group of those involved in Distance Education in Queensland, for example, to recommend that more money should be made available to install electronic equipment to facilitate individual learning and, in general, to develop what they call 'a modern communication and education delivery system'.[24] In addition, expert guidance must be provided for intending and participating students and appropriate, innovative learning packages must be devised. Whether the political will exists is, however, very much open to question.

As is apparent, TAFE colleges in Australia, like further education colleges in Britain, are increasingly being called upon to be all things to all men — and to all women. In recent years the concept of the community college has been taken up in relation to TAFE colleges in some parts of Australia,[25] which, if implemented, would, it seems, make the TAFE college more like the American Community College, in that there would be 'inter-sectoral arrangements' whereby it would offer courses currently largely restricted to the Colleges of Advanced Education, and also establish closer links with post-compulsory provision in the secondary sector. Although some TAFE colleges have been offering accredited courses of advanced education and other shorter courses, which enable their students to be granted credit for their successful completion when they subsequently enter courses in Colleges of Advanced Education and Universities, by and large the lines of demarcation between the three sectors of tertiary education have been fairly rigid. However, in the last few years there has been a softening of attitudes and, as a result, the Australian Education Council, which consists of the Minister of Education of the Commonwealth, the States and the Northern Territory, established, in January 1985, the Australian Council on Tertiary Awards (ACTA) to develop and maintain a national register of awards across tertiary education. Rather like the recently-created National Council for Vocational Qualifications in the United Kingdom, ACTA has adopted categories of awards, though more far-ranging than in the United Kingdom, numbering seven in all, from certificates, through diplomas to Bachelors' and Masters' Degrees. One of the likely effects of the creation of ACTA is to facilitate a development which is already taking place in some TAFE colleges, namely an increase in the variety and extent of the advanced courses which they presently offer.

At the level of intersection with the secondary school sector, co-operative programmes between the schools and the TAFE colleges are also expanding, though in some states they are a relatively recent innovation: in Queensland, for example, they first began in the mid-1970s with special high schools and, by 1985, 46 per cent of state high schools were involved in co-operative programmes with 21 TAFE colleges. These programmes, which bear a strong resemblance to the 'link' programmes which were fairly common in England and Wales a few years ago, are designed to give a broad introduction to a major occupational area, and they, too, may well expand over the next few years. In South Australia, also, closer links between school and TAFE have developed in recent years, to the advantage of both sectors. Joint programmes have been instituted, and some school courses grant credit for transfer into TAFE programmes and, in this way, are increasingly acting as preparatory studies for TAFE.

In general, however, the three separate sectors of tertiary education still maintain largely separate identities, with separate classifications, and funding arrangements. This 'bailiwick syndrome', as it has been dubbed by Hugh Hudson[26] Chairman of the Tertiary Education Commission, and a trenchant critic of the lack of co-operation between institutions, works to the disadvantage of a number of students. Hudson has argued publicly for more flexible arrangements for intersectoral transfers, and for new types of tertiary institutions which encompass more than one sector. As we have seen, the Community College represents a move in this direction though few, if any, successful institutions of this kind have come into being. One such is the Orana Community College in the small town of Dubbo, New South Wales, 414 kilometres north-west of Sydney. Orana, as yet the first and only community college in the state, was establshed in November 1980 and moved into a new purpose-built campus in 1983. It also has a number of satellite centres which, together with the main college, offer about 120 courses to more than 3,500 students scattered throughout the western part of the State. However, as a community college it was originally intended to provide for 'the post-secondary needs' of all the people in the area, including advanced courses. In practice, little or no advanced work is done and, as a consequence, Orana scarcely differs from other TAFE colleges. Nevertheless, in a remote town like Dubbo with no College of Advanced Education, as in many other similar towns dotted about Australia, the fully-fledged community college has much to offer and, as hopefully the firm boundary lines between the tertiary sectors become blurred, doubtless its day will come.

The quality of teaching in the TAFE colleges depends greatly on the provision of initial training and staff development programmes for TAFE teachers, and in this regard Australia is well ahead of the United Kingdom. Indeed, unlike us, all the states and territories with the exception of South Australia require their newly-appointed full-time TAFE teachers who do not already have a recognised teaching qualification, to undertake a course leading to one. As a result, of the more than 17,000 full-time TAFE teachers in Australia in 1984, about 14,000 were fully qualified, a situation which contrasts starkly with England and Wales where fewer than half our full-time further education teachers are trained. Even in South Australia there is a very strong incentive for unqualified TAFE teachers to take training courses, in the form of higher salaries and better career prospects, with the result that many do so.

The precise form of training varies from state to state but courses are most commonly run on a part-time basis for two years and lead to a TAFE teaching diploma. The courses are offered by nine Colleges of Advanced Education — two in New South Wales, and one each in the Australian Capital Territory, the Northern Territory, and the other five states — sometimes in conjunction with staff development sections of the state divisions of TAFE. In New South Wales, for example, 90 per cent of TAFE teachers are trained at The Institute of Technical and Adult Teacher Education (ITATE), which is part of Sydney College of Advanced Education, and occupies new buildings close to the centre of Sydney. The remaining 10 per cent, from the more northern parts of the state, are trained at Newcastle CAE, in the state's second city, 170 kilometres north of Sydney along the coast. The two-year course, which is overseen by the state's Teacher Education Unit, set up as recently as 1984 to promote TAFE training and staff development, operates on a block- and day-release basis. It begins with an introductory twelve week block, in which the teacher spends four days a week at ITATE and the fifth at his or her own college, and is completed by attendance at ITATE for one day a week for the rest of the first year and two days a week in the second year. A somewhat similar four-semester programme operates in Tasmania, based on the Tasmanian State Institute of Technology at Launceston, while in Victoria an 'intern model' is employed whereby newly-recruited TAFE teachers typically undertake a two-year course during which they attend the Hawthorn Institute of Education, in Melbourne, for two or three days a week, and teach in their own colleges for the rest of the week. Perhaps the most generous, and rigorous, arrangements are those which obtain in Queensland. Here, all new TAFE teachers, from whichever college they are appointed to in the state, are attached to a TAFE college in Brisbane for their first two years in order to undertake a sandwich course of training. The first six months, or semester, are spent at the state's own TAFE Teacher Preparation Centre and in their Brisbane colleges, where their work is overseen by a small group of expert and experienced tutors. In the second semester the teachers undertake full-time study, mainly of theoretical apsects of education, at the Mount Gravatt campus of the Brisbane CAE, which as the name suggests is attractively perched on the top of a hill in a Brisbane suburb. In the third semester the teachers return to their Brisbane college for further teaching and to complete a supervised curriculum project, and in the fourth semester they return to full-time study at Mount Gravatt. This course, therefore, constitutes a very thorough training programme which, like those of the other states, leads to a TAFE teacher's diploma.[27] Like any human construction, the programme is not without its critics, and its problems: for example, senior staff in TAFE colleges in parts of the state distant from Brisbane complain that no sooner have staff been appointed from their district than they lose them for two years and, indeed, once having gone to Brisbane some of them will understandably prefer to look for a post in a college in the capital city, rather than be returned to the college to which they were originally appointed.

Nevertheless this programme, like those in the other states, has much to commend it, and TAFE teachers in Australia are more generously treated in this regard than any other teachers in the country. However, initial training for TAFE teachers is very largely funded by the Commonwealth Government, with inputs from the states, and as it is a relatively expensive enterprise some doubt has been expressed about whether the funds will continue to be forthcoming on the present scale. Moreover, there are no equivalent compulsory programmes for part-time teachers in TAFE, though New South Wales is one state which has been undertaking a major survey of the training needs of part-time staff, possibly with a view to introducing mandatory programmes, while Queensland runs a voluntary programme for part-time teachers in all its colleges.

As far as experienced full-time teachers of TAFE are concerned, the state departments of TAFE have, for the most part, special staff development sections which run varied programmes of courses, lectures and conferences. Unsurprisingly, a 1980 survey of staff development in TAFE showed that experienced teachers felt that their most important need was for more up-to-date knowledge of their area of subject specialization,[28] and almost certainly the same is true of today's teachers. In addition, teachers felt that other important areas of need were the acquisition of curriculum development skills, an understanding of the nature of TAFE, counselling skills, and a knowledge of elementary administrative procedures. By and large, the latter four needs are reasonably well met by the above-mentioned programmes, but providing up-dating is a much more difficult problem. As Hall points out,[29] there are three major, virtually intractable, problems with staff development programmes in Australia, as virtually everywhere else: the needs of TAFE teachers are greater than many other teachers because of the major technological changes taking place in industry and business; virtually all staff development programmes are voluntary, so that staff can quickly lose touch with new developments in their own subject; and there are few formal arrangements between TAFE colleges and industry or business for staff exchanges or secondments. In the last respect at least, they would seem to organise these things more effectively in training establishments in Japan, where exchanges between colleges and industry and business are commonplace. Another area of need would seem to be for more provision of training programmes for staff in senior managerial and administrative positions in the TAFE colleges. There is a national Administrative Staff Training College at Mount Eliza, just south of Melbourne, in Victoria, which runs an annual programme for senior TAFE staff (rather along the lines of the Further Education Staff College at Blagdon, near Bristol) sponsored by the TAFE Council. However, its capacity is limited and attendance at courses involves a great deal of expensive travel for staff in states distant from Victoria.

Finally, mention must be made of the TAFE National Centre for Research and Development. Set up as a company in late 1981 by the State, Territory and Commonwealth Ministers for Education, it is located in a historic two-storey building with the delightful, and characteristically Australian, cast iron 'lace-work', in Payneham, a suburb of Adelaide, the capital of South Australia. It has two broad areas of activity: to undertake and encourage research and development projects that are of national significance to TAFE, and to disseminate information on research and development throughout Australia. A good example of the former is an investigation into the present system of pre-service and in-service education of full-time TAFE teachers and senior college staff, being led by Dr William Hall, the Centre's Executive Director. The research, which was due to be completed by mid-1987, should culminate in a major report which, among other things, will make recommendations on how improvements can be made to the current programmes and, significantly in these hard times, how present costs to state TAFE authorities can be reduced. In addition, the Centre has since 1985 been publishing twice a year the very useful *Australian Journal of TAFE Research and*

Development. The Centre also operates the National TAFE Clearinghouse which provides information on published documents about technical and further education in Australia. Each state and territory has its own Clearinghouse which collects the information, which is then collated by the National TAFE Clearinghouse and regularly published in its publication, *Initiatives in Technical and Further Education*.

Alongside the public sector of technical education in Australia there exists a relatively small and, as in the United Kingdom, largely undocumented, private sector. The most numerous institutions in this sector appear to be commercial, business and secretarial colleges of one sort or another which, as one would expect, are most numerous in the capital cities. As well as running basic training programmes for young school-leavers, principally girls, some of these colleges also offer specialised short courses with the help of 'consultants' brought in from business organisations for this purpose. It also appears that specialist private training agencies and institutions, in areas other than business, are increasingly being called upon by industry to supply training programmes. In addition, some professional organisations such as the Australian Institute of Management and the Sales and Marketing Institute provide training in their own particular areas.[30]

Vocational training in industry

While this chapter has concentrated very largely on the provision of vocational education by the TAFE colleges, because for the most part industry and business rely on them for this purpose, it is also the case that industry and business are themselves playing some part in the initial training and retraining of their employees. This is particularly true of the white-collar areas, and large concerns like QANTAS, Australia's international airline, and major retailing and distributive chains, have established off-the-job training and retraining for their employees. However, these seem to be very much the exception rather than the rule. For one thing, the great majority of Australian industrial and business concerns have relatively small numbers of employees, so that the country has a much higher percentage than Britain of its private employment in small firms which have little incentive to invest in the vocational training of their employees. For another, even among the larger firms, many executives seem to feel that vocational training is largely a public responsibility. This is especially so for apprenticeship and trade training; thus, it has been estimated that approximately 83 per cent of apprentices take training courses in the TAFE colleges, 16 per cent combine training in the colleges with that in off-the-job industrial training centres, and only 1 per cent receive all their training on-the-job.[31] As apprenticeship practices vary greatly from one employer to another, the fact that the vast majority of apprentices attend TAFE colleges, which provide a common core of skills, does at least ensure that minimum basic standards are achieved.

The Australian system of vocational training has come in for a great deal of criticism in recent years, including those made in a 1984 OECD Draft Report,[32] and in the influential 1985 Kirby Report. The former criticised the Australian training arrangements as being based on obsolete ideas of an industrial economy requiring relatively few professional and trade workers and large numbers of semi-skilled and unskilled workers, and considered training resources inadequate and some of the training provided to be below standard. The Kirby Report pointed to similar deficiencies, highlighted the need to ensure closer co-operation between industry and the public system of vocational training and, among other things, recommended the development of industry training centres to help overcome some of these problems. Commonwealth and state government concern about these criticisms, and the inadequate and out-dated nature of much industrial training, has led, if nothing else, to the establishment of several layers of administrative machinery. While all states already had statutory training commissions, the Commonwealth Government has funded a complementary Industry Training Services Programme, with most of the money going to the establishment of a nation-wide network of 100 Industry Training Committee (ITCs), across eighteen major industries, representing more than half the private sector work force. The functions of the ITCs, which are run by the sectors of industry which they serve, include determining the needs of industry for skilled labour, promoting systematic training, and liaising with public education and training bodies. While these are very worthy aims, their translation into effective schemes of training, and especially the introduction of training programmes in much-needed areas where as yet they scarcely exist, are much more difficult matters.

The scattered nature of the Australian population, and the vast distances between one centre of population and another, clearly pose a basic and, to an extent, an intractable problem. Long established and, in some cases, retrogressive employment practices are another barrier to the development of skilled training. For many years, for example, immigration has been seen as one major solution to recurring skill shortages, by employers and politicians alike. According to Ford,[33] this situation has worsened with the rapid changes in technology and the availability of air travel, which has enabled some Australian organisations to fly in skilled people on a regular basis to provide essential maintenance on imported high technological equipment. The long-term effects, Ford argues, are to allow Australia to escape its training responsibilities and to condemn many native-born and immigrant young people to being permanently underskilled and undertrained. Moreover, the necessity to bring in technicians skilled in high technology industries reveals the relative failure of Australia's training system to develop indigenous skills in these areas. As far as the traditional trades are concerned, the long overdue reform of training schemes, particularly apprenticeships, has frequently been made difficult by the entrenched attitudes of some of the trade unions and their insistence on the demarcation of working practices which confine many workpeople to a narrow band of skills.

Conclusions

The overrriding impression that one derives from a detailed examination of the contemporary system of vocational education and training in Australia is of the traditional nature of many of its major features, such as the heavy reliance of industry and business on the TAFE colleges to provide the bulk of training, and the emphasis which is still placed on trades apprenticeship, deriving in large part from its British inheritance. This is not to say that the TAFE colleges can, or should, be criticised for being old-fashioned; after all, as we have seen, they have come a long way in the past decade or so. Since the 1974 Kangan Report, they have ceased to be the poor relations of post-school education: their enrolments have greatly increased, for the most part they have excellent facilities and well-qualified staff, their courses are generally well-regarded and increasingly sought after, and there is a reassuring and well-deserved sense of confidence in many TAFE circles. Indeed, relative to other sectors, TAFE has received, and is still receiving, preferential financial treatment from both the Commonwealth Government and from individual states. It has not, however, been immune from the general recession.

As we have seen, the return of the Hawke Commonwealth Government for the third time in July 1987 has ushered in major structural changes in the administration of vocational education and training, notably the creation of the new enlarged Department of Employment, Education and Training, headed by John Dawkins, the former Minister for Trade. On taking office he stated that his first priority would be the achievement of greater co-ordination between education and training, involving a closer connection between the education service, industry, and the trade unions. The major aim is to produce more skilled personnel without whom Australia's economic recovery is imperilled. The implications for the TAFE system are far-reaching and include new funding arrangements by the Commonwealth Government. Their purpose is quite explicit: in the words of the ministers concerned, 'Under the new funding arrangements to be introduced from 1988 the Government will continue to place a strong emphasis on the national development of TAFE which accords a high priority to its broader economic, labour market and industry development objectives'.[34]

More specifically, the TAFE colleges will be expected to place greater emphasis on their vocational role, presumably at the expense of their provision of liberal and general education; they will be required to demonstrate 'productivity improvements and efficiency gains in the use of existing resources'; the Commonwealth Government will earmark funds for specific vocational purposes; and there will be greater industrial involvement in the work of the colleges. The Commonwealth Government also strongly believes that the TAFE colleges should more nearly tailor their vocational courses to meet the needs of industry and business, as perceived by industry and business themselves, and that they should be more entrepreneurial and enter more energetically into what they describe as the 'private fee for service training market'. The similarity between these measures and recent developments in British further education colleges is, of course, striking. In terms of student numbers, therefore, TAFE's immediate future seems assured. In respect of financial and other resources, however, it is likely to be another story. During the next few years, because of the economic crisis through which Australia has been passing, the Hawke Government is almost certain to introduce draconian cuts in government spending on the public services, including education, cuts from which TAFE will not be immune.

However, although the overall funds available for TAFE may decline in relative terms, the financial stake of the Commonwealth Government is likely to grow, through funding its schemes such as the Australian Traineeship Scheme and the Adult Training Programme. As its input of funds increases proportionally, so its leverage with the state-run TAFE systems will increase. The practical implications for TAFE mean that, among other things, they will have to develop greater financial and marketing expertise and display greater flexibility in training provision in such matters as the timing and duration of courses, and in more varied structures and administrative arrangements. The impact on the colleges of the Australian Traineeship System alone, like that of the Youth Training Scheme in the United Kingdom, will require them to provide innovative forms of training for students who at present do not use the system to any great extent, and some of whom have been alienated from traditional methods of education. If the rise in youth unemployment continues, there is also likely to be an increase in non-apprenticeship enrolments from youngsters who look upon the colleges as a last resort. As the new Adult Training Programme gets under way so it, too, will bring a significant clientele of adult trainees into the colleges.

Colleges will also have to liaise much more closely with industry than has hitherto always been the case, and if the recently-created Industry Training Committees are to be fully effective as promoters of industrial training, they, too, will have to develop close links of this kind. In any case, if the colleges are to be called upon to offer courses in areas of high technology and to offer updating and upgrading vocational courses involving the use of expensive equipment, it is unlikely that sufficient money will be forthcoming to enable them to equip themselves properly, so that they will have to turn to industry for these purposes. At the same time they must safeguard the interests and needs of the disadvantaged in society and ensure as open access as possible to their programmes. The fact that Australia is increasingly a multicultural and multilingual society, and that its work force will increasingly reflect these circumstances, poses TAFE in particular with a special challenge to provide appropriate and rigorous training programmes.

Finally, there are welcome signs that the barriers between TAFE and the other sectors of the educational system are beginning to dissolve. As we have seen, at secondary school level an increasing number of pre-vocational courses are being provided which grant credit towards the programmes offered by the TAFE colleges. As far as the other sectors of tertiary education are concerned, namely the universitites and colleges of advanced education, there is likely to be pressure for them to co-operate with the TAFE sector, both in sharing scarce resources, and in accepting more schemes of credit transfer for students who have taken appropriate courses in the TAFE colleges.[35]

Whether all the changes foreshadowed above, always assuming they come about, will necessarily produce a system of vocational education and training more suited to the country's needs is, of course, open to question. Government policy in these areas seem predicated on the assumptions that what is needed in the future is a more highly-trained work force, and that the economy will have less and less need for would-be workers with few or no skills, assumptions which have been challenged in one quarter at least.[36] Indeed, it can be argued that, largely due to technological innovation, the loss of jobs for teenagers has been most evident in skilled, attractive white-collar jobs, many of which require extended periods of vocational training. The resulting de-skilling of many middle-level occupations implies that Australia's vocational education and training system should be broadly-based, curricula should develop social and negotiating, as well as vocational, skills, and governments should support the introduction of broad-based training arrangements in industries and occupations where skills are being downgraded. If these conclusions are indeed correct, then the purveyors of vocational education and training, and especially the TAFE systems and their colleges, should endeavour to convince their political masters of their validity and reflect them in the types of courses which they offer.

Chapter three

The United States of America: A Unique Diversity

Even more perhaps than Australia, the United States of America leaves the visitor with an overriding impression of its immense size and bewildering variety. The fifty states, including Alaska and Hawaii, together occupy an area of over 3.6 million square miles, or nearly 9.5 million square kilometres, with a population estimated to be just over 237 million at the beginning of 1985. Of these, some 180 million are white, 27 million black, 15 million of Hispanic origin, and the rest from innumerable other countries and parts of the world. In keeping with its vast size, the United States exhibits an enormous range of climatic conditions and terrain, including some of the most spectacular topographical features in the world, and possesses abundant natural resources.

If I may be allowed an autobiographical comment, I have been going backwards and forwards to the United States for almost a quarter of a century, I have lived there for periods of up to a year and more, and have taught in universities and colleges in different parts of the country, and each time I visit it I am more aware of its many-faceted nature and of the dismaying difficulty of making generalisations about almost any aspect of the country's life and culture. And yet, of course, this chapter sets out to encompass within a relatively few pages a summary of its system of vocational education and training. To bring such an endeavour to within manageable proportions, I spent three months there during the summer and autumn of 1986 and concentrated on four states — California, Florida, Hawaii, and Oregon — and this chapter draws very largely on them for examples of current practice. While these states cannot, perhaps, be described as typical of the country as a whole, then neither can any other state and, at least, their broad features are to be found, *mutatis mutandis*, throughout the greater part of the country.

Fortunately, there is a great volume of literature on the American scene, and on its educational system, both by American and British authors, upon which the interested reader can draw.[1] However, very little has been written specifically on the American system of vocational education and training that is easily obtainable in the United Kingdom. One of the most recent accounts is to be found in the 1984 Report of the University of Sussex Institute of Manpower Studies, *Competence and Competition*, and while one may disagree with some of its conclusions, it nevertheless provides an accurate and informative description of the context and principal features of the American system of vocational education and training. In the circumstances, only a relatively brief analysis will be given of the social and educational context in which American vocational and educational training is set, and the greater part of the chapter will be devoted to a description of the current provision of vocational education and training.

The social and educational background

Among the more relevant aspects of American society both to its educational system and also its training system are its entrepreneurial spirit, its willingness to experiment, its generally prevailing optimism, and its openness of access — all of which, to a large extent, go hand in hand. As far as the American educational system is concerned, its most striking feature is probably its decentralised nature. As an official of the Federal Department of Education put it,[2] a little wistfuly perhaps, to an international conference on educational reform:

> It is sometimes difficult for veterans of more centralized education systems to grasp how small is the role of the American national government in education. We in Washington attempt to supply statistics and research findings, occasionally to call attention to noteworthy developments, to protect individual rights embodied in our laws and our Constitution, and to direct relatively modest sums of money to assist with the extra educational costs of children with special needs and of college students requiring financial assistance.

As far as vocational education and training are concerned, however, it goes a little further than that, as the federal government has, over the years, provided a legislative framework within which the states are given a great deal of room for manoeuvre. Following a series of federal Vocational Education Acts, the first dating back to 1963, each state is now required both to set up its own Board of Vocational Education which oversees the state system, and also to develop a five-year plan for vocational education. In return, the states receive federal funds to meet the cost of specifc parts of the plan. In the 1960s and 1970s, federal aid was considerable and, indeed, the government matched equally the amount of money spent on vocational education by the states. However, since the election of President Reagan, in 1980, federal aid has proportionately much diminished, so that at present it only constitutes about one-eighth of the total spent on vocational education in the states. Within the past few years two major acts bearing on the federal financing of specific forms of vocational education and training have been passed by Congress, the Joint Training Partnership Act (JTPA) of 1982 and the Carl D. Perkins Vocational Education Act of 1984, and the effects of this legislation will be examined later in the chapter.

As far as educational provision as a whole is concerned, including vocational education, it is the constitutional responsibility of each of the fifty states and, as each has a good deal of freedom concerning the way it organises its own provision, there are in effect fifty separate educational systems. The relatively limited influence which the federal government has over these systems is reflected in the relatively small financial input which it makes to them: in the case of Hawaii, for example, only 8 per cent of the cost of running its educational system is derived from federal funds, and a similar situation obtains in most of the other states.

The administration of education is further complicated by the fact that within the great majority of states educational responsibility, for schools in particular, is placed in the hands of smaller 'local education agencies', commonly known as school districts. Thus, although the states have always carried the constitutional responsibility for providing public education, they have generally been content to allow the school districts to run their own schools, appoint their own staff, and determine their own curricula. In addition, most of the money for running the schools has traditionally been raised at local level by the school districts themselves. These vary enormously in size, from the Los Angeles School District, for example, covering the central part of the sprawling conurbation, with a school population of the order of two million, to quite small ones with school populations of perhaps only 10,000. During the present century, there has been an understandable trend to consolidate small school systems with the result that the number of school districts has steadily declined from over 40,000 in 1960 to 15,747 in the autumn of 1983. The number of school districts within individual states also varies considerably, from a substantial number in some of the larger mid-western states to only one in Hawaii where it is conterminous with the geographical borders of the state.

However, in recent years there has been a trend over much of the country for the states themselves, through their state boards of education and similar state-wide administrative machinery, to assume greater powers.[3] The two main reasons for this trend have been public concern over the standards of education in the schools, a concern which has fuelled the so-called 'Back to Basics' movement with its emphasis on improving standards of literacy and numeracy; and the growing costs of education which have particularly affected the poorer school districts. Traditionally, the greater part of the money to run the school system has been raised by school districts from property taxes, with the inevitable consequence that more affluent school districts have been able to pay higher salaries and provide better facilities, and thereby attract better teachers. The greatest contrasts in these respects have been between the affluent 'white' suburbs and the 'black' and 'Hispanic' inner city areas. In order to even out the gross inequalities which this system has brought about, many states now provide school districts with a substantial proportion of their funds. They also increasingly prescribe new rules and standards for school curricula and student achievement.

The precise duration of compulsory schooling varies somewhat from state to state and, although the irreducible minimum is nine years, from age 7 to 16, almost everywhere it runs from age 6 — usually preceded by kindergarten — and in some states the school-leaving age is 17, or even 18. Indeed, in 1980, no less than 87 per cent of the American school population was enrolled in school for a twelve-year period, from 5 to 17, and about 75 per cent 'graduated' from high school, at age 18, or in some cases at 17. The way in which the school system itself is structured also varies somewhat from state to state, though three patterns are in common use. (Figure 3.1). Perhaps the most usual is the '6-3-3' form, that is six years of elementary (or primary) school from ages 6 to 12, followed by three years of Junior High School, and three years of Senior High School, to age 18. The other two patterns are '8-4', eight years of elementary school and four years of high school; and '6-6', six years of elementary school, followed by six years of high school. Whatever the form of school organisation, vocational education is an integral part of secondary education, and is available, only on an optional or 'elective' basis, to all students.

So far we have dealt exclusively with the public system of schooling, but running alongside it is a private sector, which has grown somewhat in recent years. At the present time there are more than 20,000 private schools throughout the country, made up of predominantly Roman Catholic 'parochial' schools and private fee-paying schools run for profit, which are attended by about 11 per cent of the school population. Although there has been a growing tendency for white parents in particular to send their children to private schools, the latter are much less influential in educational circles and in public life generally than the private sector in the United Kingdom.

The provision of vocational education and training

The current picture of American provision of vocational education and

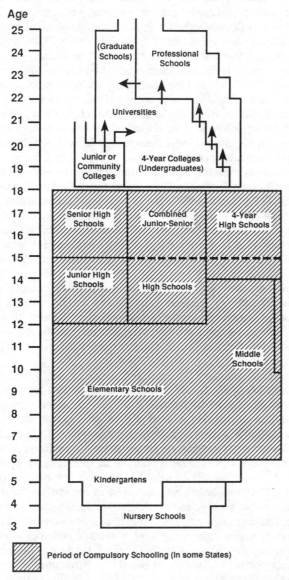

Age

25
24
23
22
21
20
19
18
17
16
15
14
13
12
11
10
9
8
7
6
5
4
3

(Graduate Schools)

Professional Schools

Universities

Junior or Community Colleges

4-Year Colleges (Undergraduates)

Senior High Schools

Combined Junior-Senior

4-Year High Schools

Junior High Schools

High Schools

Middle Schools

Elementary Schools

Kindergartens

Nursery Schools

Period of Compulsory Schooling (In some States)

Figure 3.1 The educational system in the United States of America

training is a very complex one and is the product both of a long history and also of the work of numerous agencies, sometimes co-operating and at others competing with one another. In broad terms one may distinguish between the publicly- and the privately-funded provision. The former consists of two separate systems which co-exist and, to a degree, overlap. On the one hand, there is the traditional vocational education offered mainly by the public schools and the community colleges, funded very largely by the states themselves, with some federal assistance. These insitutions provide the great bulk of such training. On the other, there are various manpower-training programmes which began in the 1960s in response to specific social and economic needs, and which have developed since then into institutions largely distinct from the public schools and community colleges. These programmes are currently funded by the Federal Government under the terms of the 1982 Job Training Partnership Act (JTPA) and the 1984 Carl D. Perkins Vocational Education Act, and their form and content are largely determined by explicit federal policies. Privately funded provision also falls into two main divisions: that provided by 'proprietary' colleges and training institutions, run mainly for profit, and that financed by industry and business and provided mainly 'in-house'.

For convenience, we shall deal first with what can broadly be described as the educational institutions, both public and private, which offer vocational education and training; then with the federally-funded institutions offering manpower training programmes; and finally with training financed by industry and business to meet its own specific requirements.

According to the American Vocational Association (AVA), a national body which, together with its affiliated state associations, represents practising vocational education teachers, teacher educators, administrators, counsellors and others involved in vocational education, more than seventeen million Americans are enrolled at any one time in public and private vocational institutions, of whom about 15.6 million are in public vocational programmes. This represents an enormous growth in enrolments over the past twenty years; however, in some parts of the country at least, there has been a slight decline in the last few years. The institutions, which number more than 26,000 across the country, fall mainly into three broad groups: high schools, area vocational centres, and post-secondary institutions of one sort or another including Community Colleges and Technical Institutes (Table 3.1). As can be seen, by far the largest number of institutions offering programmes of vocational education are the country's public *high schools*. The great majority of these are general, comprehensive schools offering a wide range of courses, of which only a percentage are vocational, though they include over 200 vocational high schools which specialise and offer only vocational programmes. The progammes offered by the high schools are usually classified into two categories: general vocational programmes, and occupational-specific programmes. The former are commonly available in grades 9 and 10, that is to 14- and 15-year-olds, and include pre-vocational courses designed to introduce students to broad occupational areas such as agriculture or business, and including such subjects as typing, home economics, and 'industrial arts', or workshop practice, which approximates to our Craft, Design and Technology. Most American high school students undertake one or more of these general vocational courses and together they account for about 65 per cent of students on all vocational programmes in high schools. The other 35 per cent fall into the occupational-specific area and these courses, which are generally provided to the eleventh and twelfth grades (aged 16 and 17) prepare students for employment in a particular occupation such as computer programming, motor mechanics, electronics or practical nursing. More specifically, in the case of Hawaii's high schools, for example, which are reasonably typical of the country as a whole, thirty-two specific courses are available under eight general 'clusters': Agriculture; Electrical and Electronic Engineering; Office Occupations, including Computer Programming and Shorthand and Typing; Marketing, including Advertising, Business Management, and Distribution; Home Economics, including Child Care services; Technical Graphics; Mechanical Occupations, including Automobile Engineering; and Construction. Clearly, because of the range of courses involved, and the expensive equipment required, no one high school is able to offer all eight clusters. The aim of these courses is to develop in students what is called 'entry level proficiency', which will enable them to make a beginning in an occupational field. As far as the students themselves are concerned, their reasons for undertaking vocational programmes are many and varied: they may have a genuine liking and aptitude for them, they may presume that they will enable them more easily to secure a job, some may wish to please their parents, and others may simply stay on at high school after school-leaving age, whether on academic or vocational courses, or both, to enjoy a more vigorous social life, or to avoid the physical dangers of street life in some of America's large cities.

Because of the expense of equipping all public high schools to teach vocational courses, and because good teachers of the subject are in very short supply, a number of school districts have established vocational high schools which usually draw their students from the catchment areas of anything from two to five secondary schools. They have spread so widely that there are now about 2,000 of them in the country and they are to be found in every state except Hawaii, North Carolina and Wyoming, though Hawaii for some time has been considering establishing at least one. Their average size is small as American public schools go,

Table 3.1 Vocational education in the United States

Type of institution	Number of institutions	Number of students (approx.)
		('000,000)
Public		
General high schools	15,729	
Vocational high schools	225	9.3
Area vocational centers	1,395	
Community colleges/technical institutes	1,190	6.3
Skill centres[1]	70	
	18,609	15.6
Private		
Secondary schools	586	
Post secondary institutions	6,813	1.5
Correspondence	83	
	7,482	
Total	26,091	17.1

(Source: American Vocational Education Fact Sheet, *Vocational Education Today*, 1987)
[1] These institutions specialize in providing programmes for economically disadvantaged students.

having only between 400 and 500 students, and they recruit mainly high school students, who make up about 85 per cent of their population, and some adults. They offer both broad vocational education and occupational specific courses, in the ratio of 52:48, and some of them offer courses in connection with the Job Training Partnership Act. The recruitment of adults into these courses is thus widespread and in California, for example, they are also catered for in what are known as Adult Schools, which concentrate on specific job training with the goal of rapid employment. Elsewhere, classes in the vocational high schools may either contain high school students and adults separately, or mix them together. A small proportion of these vocational high schools has acquired excellent reputations, especially those in the large cities which recruit students across a large area and develop reputations for excellence in certain specific vocational areas. Not surprisingly, many of their graduates move on to undertake degree courses in vocational subjects in high quality colleges and universities. However, the 'dual system' as it is sometimes called, that is the co-existence of general and vocational high schools, is not without its critics. While conceding that the vocational high schools have much going for them, they nevertheless point to the additional cost which their laboratories and equipment entail, the social segregation that occurs when teachers and students attend separate schools, one called vocational and the other academic, and the curriculum segregation which is inevitably involved.[4] With the increasing emphasis that is currently being placed on academic high school graduation requirements, the future for some vocational high schools may be problematical. While a limited number of specialised high schools may be highly regarded by society at large, the same is certainly not true of high school vocational education in general. For example, a recent, important and trenchant report on the role of vocational education in America's high school, entitled *The Unfinished Agenda*[5], castigates what it calls 'the educational myopia' which pervades American society and downgrades and assigns second-class status to high school vocational education. One consequence of this widespread attitude is, for example, that some of the most successful high school courses, in areas like business studies and computer programming, are only reluctantly listed as such. Another familiar problem, in the United States as in the world over, is that teachers of vocational education are, in the words of the report, 'underpaid, underprepared and asked to work miracles', and, as a result, an increasing number of the best of them are leaving the profession. Nor does it come as any surprise to learn that the report identifies enormous inequities in the quality of courses and teaching between affluent suburban high schools and less affluent inner-city and rural schools, nor that disadvantaged students are not represented in vocational programmes in proportion to their incidence in the general population, nor that 'sex-linked enrolment patterns' resist most efforts to change them, with males found mostly in such areas as 'trade and industrial' and females in 'office and clerical'.[6]

Another very interesting survey of public vocational education in California, entitled *One Million Hours A Day*,[7] highlights the difficulty which high schools find in providing up-to-date equipment for vocational courses from their relatively meagre funds, and points to the fact that as their teaching staff are full-time and permanent, the schools lack flexibility in deploying staff to meet the changing demands of the marketplace for specific skills. It contends that high school vocational courses are not 'demonstrably effective' in helping students to find jobs after they graduate, nor in retraining would-be drop-outs. It concludes that they would be better advised to cease trying to provide skill training for entry-level jobs, a task which it argues they are not well situated to do, and instead concentrate on giving young people a broad vocational education which will promote learning, problem-solving and communication skills. Other writers on the subject foresee that high schools will have to move in this direction, willy-nilly, because of the increasing difficulty of keeping equipment, curriculum and teachers up-to-date with rapidly changing technology.[8] These, however, are merely particular views in a wide-ranging, and often heated, debate about the future role of vocational education in the public high schools,[9] and *The Unfinished Agenda*, for example, sees a broad remit for high school vocational education, which should both provide general skills and also develop job-specific ones. Its principal concern is to correct the lack of quality which is endemic to much vocational education in the high schools and, to this end, has valuable suggestions to make, including greater student access, an improved curriculum, better articulation with post-secondary vocational education, and improved teacher recruitment and preparation. To implement these changes would require political will, at national and state levels, and the infusion of a great deal of money; unfortunately, there is little indication that either will be forthcoming in the foreseeable future.

In the meantime, in some areas of the country the numbers of students on vocational courses have declined, and one major reason for this is that as states have sought to respond to the 'Back to Basics' movement and generally improve the standards of high school students by increasing the requirements for 'graduation' in academic areas, so less time has become available for 'electives' such as vocational education. Moreover, this reduction of the time available for vocational courses has coincided in many parts of the country with the concentration of these courses in area or regional centres of one sort or another, numbering almost 1,400 in all. An interesting example of one type of regional centre is to be found in California in the shape of its *Regional Occupation Centers and Programs* or ROC/ROPs for short. These centres, which number sixty-seven, are mainly in the large towns, unlike New York State which has similar centres but which locates them outside of the towns. In California, where they occupy various accommodation, sometimes within the high schools themselves, they catered for 139,000 students in the academic year 1983–4, of whom 100,000 were high school students in grades 11 and 12, and 39,000 were adults. By comparison, in the same year, California's high schools enrolled 234,000 eleventh and twelfth grade students and its Community Colleges recruited about 700,000 students on vocational education programmes. An important characteristic of ROC/ROP programmes, which are now more than twenty years old, is that attendance is entirely voluntary: in some cases, students spend the morning in their high school and the afternoon in the ROC/ROP, or vice versa, and in others attendance at the latter occurred in the evenings or weekends, after a full high school programme. The ROC/ROPs are closely scrutinised by the State Department of Education which finances them and approves their courses. However, as they receive no federal funds they are not subject to federal regulations regarding social and working conditions which may be something of a mixed blessing. The amount of money they get is closely related to the numbers of students they enrol, so that their directors have to be entrepreneurial in the best American tradition and convince would-be students that, having completed their courses, their prospects of getting a job are enhanced, as indeed seems to be the case. It also means that the directorate must be in close touch with the skill requirements of local industry. From a management point of view, the director of a ROC/ROP has more flexibility than the principal of a high school, particularly concerning the deployment of staff. Thus, he will usually have a large number of staff who are part-time and/or on fixed term appointments, he will pay lower salaries than the high school, and his staff will include a larger proportion of blacks, Hispanics and women. Many of his part-time staff will also be working in occupations related to the courses they teach. In general, staff in the ROC/ROPs will be 'less established in the teaching profession but probably more established in the occupations they teach' than comparable staff in the high schools.[10] On the whole the centres seem to be well stocked with equipment, for which they receive more generous grants than do the high schools. Although they offer a similarly wide range of job-specific courses, they tend to concentrate on nursing, retailing and construction, possibly at a more advanced level than the high schools. They also place rather more emphasis on tailoring their courses to ensure their 'graduates' obtain jobs and less on their attainment of broader skills and competencies. By and large, the ROC/ROPs seem to have done a good job during the past twenty years or so of their existence, and are generally well thought of in the state capital, Sacramento, where a well-organised lobby has operated very successfully on their behalf. One by-product of their success in attracting substantial numbers of high school students is that a number of California's high schools have cut down on their own vocational education programmes.

Perhaps the most important publicly-funded educational institutions providing vocational education below degree level are the *Community Colleges* and *Technical Institutes*, which number almost 1,200 across the country. Some confusion arises from the fact that they are known under a variety of terms in different parts of the country: in the southern states for example, the term 'technical institute' is widely used, partly because some of them concentrate very largely on vocational programmes, and elsewhere they may be called city colleges, junior colleges, or technical colleges. However, the term 'community college' is the most common one and, for that reason, will be used in this chapter. Although some of them have been in existence for a fairly long period, most of them have been established only in the past twenty-five years, in response to growing public demand. During that period their enrolments have increased considerably — in 1979, for example, 51 per cent of all college students were enrolled in community colleges, compared with 21 per cent in 1965[11] — though in California, with the greatest number of community colleges in the country, enrolments have declined in the last three or four years.

The community colleges are known as 'two-year colleges' in that they award qualifications after the equivalent of two years' full-time study, or less, a span of time which distinguishes them from universities and colleges offering four-year courses which lead to baccalaureate degrees. Broadly speaking, their two main functions are to provide two-year 'transfer' courses, and one-year, or shorter, vocational courses. The former are available either in the liberal arts or in the sciences, and lead to the award of what are often called Associate Degrees. Having successfully completed these courses, a student may then transfer, under the American credit system, to a further two years in a university or four-year college in order to obtain a bachelor's degree, hence the term 'transfer' courses. Though many of the two-year courses are in the liberal arts, others are clearly vocational in nature. The second major group of students consists of those undertaking the equivalent of one-year full-time courses, or less, sometimes linked to apprenticeships, which lead to the award of certificates in a wide variety of vocational and technical fields. In addition, the Community Colleges offer a variety of other programmes, including language and citizen training for immigrants, basic education skills for undereducated adults, and cultural enrichment for their communities. The colleges pride themselves on their 'open access', in offering courses to anyone who wishes to attend. Many of their students attend courses on a part-time basis, while holding down a full-time job and while, in a typical college, the average age of the students arithmetically is about 28, the most numerous are those aged 21 or 22. They are also essentially 'commuter colleges', with most students living at home and travelling to and from the college daily. In appearance, the average American community college is like one of our more recently-built colleges of further education and, in function, it has been compared, with some justice, to the British tertiary college.[12]

The largest system of community colleges in the United States is to be found in California where there are no fewer than 106 of them, recruiting annually over 1,150,000 students, of whom approximately 700,000 are undertaking vocational courses. On average, therefore, each Californian community college has more than 10,000 students, while in the large cities student populations frequently exceed 20,000. This large size enables them to offer a considerable range of vocational programmes and to render viable even highly specialised technical courses. Many of these are tailor-made to meet the needs of local industry and business which funds them, especially in subject areas such as the installation of television sets and satellite discs, and in welding. For example, in a particular college in Long Beach, which is part of the greater Los Angeles conurbation, a range of 'non-credit' courses is offered for employees in the local McDonnell Douglas aircraft industry, in the local shipyards, and in telephone, communications, and word-processing companies. Some of these courses take the form of adult retraining, which has become a major issue in the United States. In California itself, the state has set up an Employment Training Panel which contracts with community colleges and other institutions to provide specific programmes which it then finances, although opinions about the worth and quality of these programmes are sharply divided. As we have seen, colleges are also involved in apprenticeship training, either through federal or state programmes which lay down requirements for off-the-job study. These programmes are for both trade union members and for 'non-union' employers. Most trade unions run their own courses in their own training centres but, to an extent, draw upon the expertise in the colleges. 'Non-union' workshops and employers, however, generally lack these facilities and, especially in Oregon for example, turn to the colleges for help. The situation is made more complicated by the fact that some employers across the country, opposed to the job demarcation which is often strongly protected by the traditional unions, have created their own unions, a trend which seems to be on the increase. The community colleges also have a major responsibilty for offering courses in high technology areas which involve the purchase of expensive equipment and which, for this reason, are largely neglected by the private institutions. Thus, despite a grave shortage of funds, a typical community college in southern California has recently spent a great deal of money on computers, robots, and various types of digital equipment.

Like the further education colleges in the United Kingdom, California's community colleges offer vocational courses to minority groups and provide a 'safety net' for students who drop out of high school. As we have seen, they have traditionally welcomed all students, aged 18 or over, who have the ability to benefit from their courses regadless of their prior schooling or their lack of a high school diploma. As a result, low income students and disadvantaged ethnic minority youth are better represented in California's community colleges than in the state universities or on the campuses of the University of California. But even there they are under-represented: within five years of leaving high school, 29.3 per cent of all 15-year-old high school students will have enrolled in a California community college programme compared to 26.2 per cent of black students and only 18.8 per cent of Hispanic origin.[13] Nevertheless, it is to the great credit of the colleges that 80 per cent of all 'under-represented' students who enter post-secondary education courses in the state come in through their doors.[14]

In recent years, the Californian community colleges have faced a number of severe difficulties and have also come under much closer public scrutiny. Among their greatest problems have been the shortage of funds with which to buy the latest equipment and to ensure that their libraries are well-stocked with up-to-date literature; the difficulty in recruiting good, highly-qualified staff, which is partly due to the fact that in some quarters they are still regarded as 'glorified high schools'; and the difficulty in assessing, counselling and placing students on relevant and appropriate courses. Partly for these reasons, the Californian community colleges have not found favour with the present Governor, George Deukmejian, who has criticised them for their 'lack of quality' and for failing to give students proper counselling in order to channel good ones into challenging work and to encourage poorer ones to do better. The Governor, scenting the political wind, has been articulating a strong feeling in some quarters that community college students have been encouraged to enrol on a very wide range of courses, some of little value, often with little guidance, with the result that there has been a high drop-out and a low 'transfer' rate, especially for students with language difficulties or learning deficiencies. For various reasons the community colleges have in recent years received more and more money from the state, so that, inevitably perhaps, he who pays the piper wishes to call the tune. Moreover, the 106 colleges, which are spread over seventy local districts, are each governed by a local-elected Board of Trustees which, often with good reason, determines individual policies for each institution, a feature which has, however, found little favour in Sacramento. Consequently, a Commission for the Review of the Master Plan for Higher Education in California, first set up in 1960, was recreated in 1984 to recommend changes in public post-secondary education in the state, namely in the University of California, the state universities, and the community colleges. The last-named were given the highest priority and the Commission's Report, *The Challenge of Change: A Reassessment of the California Community Colleges*, duly appeared in March 1986. It makes no fewer than 68 recommendations, many of them relating to vocational courses: among them, that stringent efforts should be made to increase the representation of under-privileged groups; that closer articulation should be effected with high schools, on the one hand, and with the universitites on the other; that the colleges should work more closely with local business and industry by offering more 'employer-specific contract education programs'; and that some colleges should be able to apply to be designated as 'technical colleges' specialising in vocational education and training.[15] At the time of writing, the Report has been followed up by some limited legislation, which has not increased state control to the extent that some would wish. However, in April 1986 the state appointed a Chancellor to lead the 106 community colleges and secure a degree of state-wide co-ordination.

By contrast, a high degree of state-wide control of vocational education has long been a feature in Hawaii. Here, in 1968, the governing body of the University of Hawaii was designated the State Board of Vocational Education, so that the six community colleges in the state are, in effect, part of the University system, though Presidents of the community colleges have powers to start new courses and employ staff. In theory, at least, this administrative arrangement, which is also to be found in a number of other states such as Kentucky and Wisconsin, ensures a co-ordinated and effective state-wide system of post-secondary education.

The changes in policy regarding community colleges in California, especially the concern to improve the quality of courses they offer and to reduce student wastage, are also to be found in Hawaii and, to varying extents, are also mirrored in many other parts of the country.[16] However, among America's community colleges and technical institutes are a number which can claim 'o be among the most interesting and most lively educational institutions in the country. Colleges in this category respond very quickly to the needs of local industry and set up specialist programmes such as those offered by the Robotics Research Center at the Piedmost Technical College in Greenville, South Carolina, which is located there partly because it is close to one of America's largest manufacturers of robots. Another example of a community college much concerned with meeting the training needs of local industry is the Niagara County Community College in New York State which, in 1986, enrolled well over 26,000 local employees in specially designed training programmes. This sort of development owes much to individual enterprise at both college and state level and, as a result, some colleges have become very large institutions indeed. Among the most highly regarded is the Miami Dade Community College in Southern Florida which operates on no fewer than four campuses and several 'outreach' centres offering courses to tens of thousands of students. Among the courses it offered for the first time in the academic session 1986–7 were a new micro-computer services programme, a certificate course for students wishing to become nannies, and a special orientation programme for women interested in becoming fire rescue workers. Thus, the range of courses in an institution of this sort is almost infinite and the college as a whole exhibits an enviable vitality.

Of considerable importance in the spectrum of American provision of vocational education and training is that made by what we would call *the private sector*, namely proprietorial colleges and schools operating very largely for profit. However, as in many other instances, there is a confusion of terminology between the two countries in that in America the term 'private sector' is generally taken to mean the private sector of industry and business which, of course, is much involved in providing its own training as well as contracting it out to both public and proprietorial training institutions. To avoid confusion, therefore, the term 'proprietorial institutions' will be used in this chapter. Other than a relatively small number of private secondary schools which offer vocational programmes much like those in their public counterparts, the comprehensive high schools, proprietorial institutions consist very largely of vocational colleges of one sort or another: as they number more than 6,800 across the country and annually recruit more than one-and-a-half million students, they represent very big business indeed. Described in Federal Government statistics under the umbrella term 'non-college postsecondary schools with occupational programs', they assume various titles, often reflecting the range of courses or occupational specialities they offer. Thus, many of them come under the general title 'Trade and Technical Schools', some of which date back to colonial times, while others style themselves variously Business Schools or Paramedical Colleges. To British observers the confusion is confounded because, in popular parlance, an American student when he says he is attending 'school' uses the term to denote a post-secondary institution, be it community college, state college, or university.

The proprietorial vocational colleges, then, by and large, only offer courses in specific occupational areas and, unlike community colleges, are not concerned with general education. They are 'authorised' or 'approved' by the state, provided they meet certain minimum criteria, and they award certificates and diplomas, many of which can be obtained in a relatively short time, and which, for the most part are accredited by a variety of national and state-wide agencies. Among the national accrediting bodies, for example, are the National Association of Trade and Technical Schools, and the National Bureau of Health Education Schools. In California, as in other states, there are state-wide groupings such as the California Association of Private Post-Secondary Schools, which operates a political lobby in Sacramento, the state capital, on behalf of its members; the California Barber College Association; and the California Association of Schools of Cosmetology. So many and varied are these colleges and their groupings that, as one report puts it, 'If there is a market in California, it seems that some enterprising educational entrepreneur has already filled it'.[17]

In fact, however, California, relative to its size and population, is not particularly well-endowed with proprietorial colleges as the public institutions are numerous and easily accessible. On the other hand, its northern neighbour, Oregon, has made less provision for public vocational education, so that students turn instead to the private sector. In general, it appears that proprietorial colleges are more strongly represented on the east coast of the country than the west coast. Like their counterparts in the United Kingdom and Australia, statistical information about their enrolments and programmes is in short supply and accurate figures are apparently almost impossible to obtain. However, a Californian survey of 1984 which attempted to gauge their size and scope calculated that in 1982 they enrolled over 460,000 students and that among the most common institutions were business and secretarial colleges, and beauty schools. In addition, in recent years there has been a rapid growth in colleges offering training in computer programming, data processing and courses for air-conditioning mechanics.[18] Although in the past many of them received a good deal of federal financial assistance, this no longer seems to be the case and, partly for this reason, they tend to concentrate on the less capital intensive programmes.

As the result of a small and very limited survey of proprietorial institutions in California and Florida in the summer of 1986, I concluded that for the most part they fell into three broad categories: business and secretarial schools — including courses in computing and word processing; technical and trade schools which together offered a very wide range of courses, including not only the 'traditional' trades, but also travel and tourism, and short courses in such subjects as Bar Tending and Poodle Grooming; and colleges which specialised in training personnel for the Paramedical professions. However, specific colleges may well offer a wide range of courses, and a typical one in a large Florida city, which styles itself a 'National College of Technology', offers programmes in computer programming, microcomputer-operating, medical data processing, travel and tourism, and two-year courses in computer programming and cardio-vascular technology, leading to Associate Degrees recognised by the state of Florida. The college itself is accredited by several national accrediting bodies. All these courses were available on a full-time and a part-time basis and they are often available on a year-round basis. Courses are frequently revised to ensure they are up-to-date and the schools employ many teachers from industry.[19] The proprietorial colleges can also be said to have certain features in common which distinguish them from the community colleges, with which, of course, they are in competition for students. They claim to enable their students to complete similar courses in a shorter time: in Oregon, for example, a course for motor mechanics takes 60 per cent of the time taken by a similar one in a nearby community college; they are much more expensive than the public institutions; and they claim to be much more successful in placing their graduates in jobs. Although there is some evidence to support this last contention — as it is a major selling point, some colleges go to great trouble to place their products all over the country — it remains a matter of some dispute. Partly because of the expense, the colleges suffer from a high wastage rate, and many students drop out of their courses and go back in again, as and when they raise the money to continue. Many of the colleges are popular with students from the ethnic minorities, partly because they advertise their wares much more assiduously than the public institutions, and partly because they place very few bureaucratic obstacles in the way of students who wish to enrol in them.

Like the Special Training Schools in Japan, they are very responsive to labour market demands and seek to find out the needs of industry and business and to cater for them. Because their continued existence depends to a large extent on placing their graduates in jobs, they work very closely with local employers and frequently tailor their programmes to their particular specifications. Although the proprietary vocational schools have, on the whole, been very successful in the last decade or two, not all of them flourish, and a proportion come and go after only a few years existence. Inevitably, they are very variable in quality and have some of the best and worst examples of American vocational and education and training. None the less, their very numbers ensure that, unlike their counterparts in the United Kingdom and Australia, they make a major contribution to the American training system.

Finally, mention must be made of one other group of educational institutions in the United States which offers programmes of vocational education, namely the eighty recognised Correspondence Schools. These schools, which have their own accrediting body, concentrate on trade and industrial courses in such areas as motor mechanics, metal-working, and construction; and also on courses for people working or wishing to work in the distribution industry.[20] A number of these schools employ recent technological developments such as learning by video disc, and it seems likely that both the use of these methods and also the overall number of correspondence schools will increase in the future. However, given that the vast majority of Americans are within reasonable commuting distance of one institution or another providing vocational education and training, they are unlikely to rival the Australian distance learning network proportionately in size.

As we have seen, the concern of the Federal Government to ensure that the country's manpower needs are met has mainly taken the form of funding the provision of vocational education and training by various agencies within the states. A steady stream of acts passed by Congress has laid down the rules by which the states can obtain federal funds and among the most important of these was, until fairly recently, the Comprehensive Employment and Training Act (CETA), which was passed in 1973 and lasted for nine years until it was superseded by the Job Training Partnership Act (JTPA) of 1982. CETA funds were made available for youth training and youth employment to what were called 'Prime Sponsors', that is, various combinations of educational establishments, the private sector of industry, and state organisations and agencies. As a result, a whole range of programmes came into being, offered by multifarious bodies, both public and private. The programmes were largely directed at unemployed youngsters of whom, as in the United

Kingdom, a disproportionate number were from ethnic minorities and other disadvantaged groups. In 1986, for example, the unemployment rate among disadvantaged young people was running nationally at about 40 per cent. In many ways CETA programmes were not unlike those provided under the aegis of the British Youth Opportunities Programme and were criticised on similar grounds: that the quality of many of them was too low, that too few of those who completed them obtained jobs, that the trainees were being used by employers as cheap labour, and that they were a drain on federal resources. With the coming into office of President Reagan, the political and economic climate changed, and the Federal Government's avowed belief in 'states' rights' was translated into making it clear to them that they must solve their own training problems and largely finance their own programmes. Accordingly, CETA was replaced by the Job Training Partnership Act of 1982, with a substantially reduced federal budget. The Act, which went into operation in October 1983, bears the conservative stamp of the Reagan administration in two ways:[21] it reduces the amount of federal funding, very largely by eliminating CETA's principal component, the creation of employment in public services; and it stresses state and local control and the involvement of industry, unlike CETA's administration, which was mainly under the control of the Federal Department of Labor. The programmes funded by JTPA are specifically designed for training unskilled and other disadvantaged young people and adults, and the money goes to the governors of the states who are required to establish Service Delivery Areas (SDA), of which there are currently 579 across the country. Each SDA appoints a Private Industry Council (PIC) — these existed previously, but they are now required to contain a majority of private sector employers among their members — which plans the administration and organisation of training in its locality and contracts with various agencies to provide it. Experience in some states such as Oregon has shown that few SDAs have turned to community colleges to provide training, mainly because they place a high priority on short-term on-the-job training programmes which they perceived the colleges are unable or unwilling to offer. Instead, they turn to industry and to community-based and regional consortia of agencies to provide job training services. In any case, JTPA, unlike CETA, is supposed to be 'performance-driven', that is the training contractors have, in many cases, to demonstrate that their trainees obtain jobs or they do not get paid.[22] Moreover, over the few years since JTPA was introduced, progressively less federal money has been forthcoming for its programmes.

Given that, unlike the United Kingdom's Youth Training Scheme, there is no one national JTPA scheme, that states are not obliged to avail themselves of federal funds for this purpose, and that a multiplicity of agencies and institutions, both public and private, are involved in providing training programmes whose content inevitably varies considerably, it seems difficult either to assess the progress that has been made under the Act or to generalise about its impact across the country as a whole. However, over a period of twenty-five years or so, a network of manpower training programmes has developed, currently funded under JTPA, largely separate from the vocational education programmes in high schools and community colleges, and run mainly by a large range of separate bodies and institutions, involving state agencies, local government officials, the business community, and local community-based organisations, among others. Inevitably, perhaps, this network of provision forms the bottom tier of American vocational training and, although some JTPA programmes in every state are of high quality, many of them have low status and leave much to be desired. Because JTPA-sponsored institutions are designed to serve low-income minority groups, it seems that in the words of a percipient reviewer of their progress, 'Political, economic, organizational and social factors all conspire to make such segregated institutions almost inherently unequal'.[23] It comes as no surprise to learn that they have difficulty in recruiting good staff, that they are subject to constant political and organizational changes, and that securing employment for their trainees is a major problem. Moreover, despite the fact that the Private Industry Councils have a majority of their members from industry and business, ensuring sound relationships between those administering the programmes and private industry has turned out to be difficult: industry tends to shy away from the bureaucratic procedures that have grown up and, frequently, does not want to be too closely involved with what it sees as low-prestige activities. Hopefully, however, these attitudes will change, and co-operation between industry and business, on the one hand, and the providers of vocational education and training, on the other, will grow.

It is one of the major objectives of the Carl D. Perkins Vocational Education Act of 1984, named after the late Carl Perkins, a Kentucky Congressman, and for many years a powerful advocate of federal aid to vocational education and training, to promote co-operation of this kind. To this end, it requires the states who wish to participate to establish State Councils on Vocational Education with a majority of their members, including the chairman, from the private sector. More significantly, perhaps, it specifies that individual State Plans for Vocational Education, which have been in existence for some time, should both 'assess the current and future needs for job skills' within each state and also 'assess the quality of vocational education in terms of the pertinence of programs to the workplace and to new and emerging technologies and the responsiveness of programs to current and projected occupational needs in each state'. As a result, many states have developed increasingly complex and sophisticated manpower planning and vocational programming systems. However, translating these into actual courses in the colleges is another, and much more difficult, matter. The Perkins Act also encourages the establishment of partnerships between industry and education in promoting the design of programmes and curricula, 'especially tailored to the needs of an industry or group of industries for skilled workers'. However, in comparison to its predecessors, the main thrust of the Perkins Act is to narrow the purpose of its basic state grant programme to two specific areas: ensuring that individuals, presently inadequately served by vocational education programmes, have access to provision of quality; and helping the states to improve and expand their provision of good vocational programmes. Thus, it devotes more than half its funds to 'special populations', mainly disadvantaged and handicapped individuals, including those with limited English proficiency; adults in 'need of training, retraining or upgrading'; 'homemakers' and single parents; and individuals participating in programmes designed to eliminate 'sex bias and stereotyping'.

As the Perkins Act only came into effect on July 1985, it is too early fully to assess its effects. However, it is one of the requirements of the Act that the federal Department of Education submits to Congress regular assessments of the national condition of vocational education and its first such report, *Design Papers for the National Assessment of Vocational Education*, has only recently been published. Although, as its title suggests, it is much concerned with putting forward criteria and methodologies by which to make the assessment, it does cast much illumination on recent developments in the field. It is, however, noncommittal about the effectiveness to date of the Perkins Act and one cannot but feel that like its predecessors, it will find it very difficult to make much progress in a very complex field.

Finally, although JTPA and the Carl Perkins Act are currently at the centre of federal efforts to encourage work-related education and training, they are not the only ones. For example, a substantial proportion of federal aid goes as financial help to individual students, many of whom are on vocational education programmes. However, whatever the precise direction in which funds are directed, overall there has been a cumulative series of cuts in recent years which undoubtedly has had an impact, and a largely adverse one, on the provision of vocational education and training nationally. Indeed, the Reagan administration wishes to go further than it has done hitherto and, at the time of writing, is contemplating cutting back the federal appropriation to vocational education in 1987 and ending it in 1988. Its grounds for doing so, according to the Department of Education, are that most states have reached or are approaching 'self-sufficiency' in vocational education, a dubious assumption at best.

Vocational training in industry

As in Japan, the amount of training provided and funded by industry and business is enormous, estimated to be roughly equivalent in terms of the numbers of employers involved to the entire educational system in the United States.[24] Until fairly recently, little accurate information was available on the subject: for example, the first systematic inquiry ever undertaken into the scope and character of corporate education and development activities was published in 1977[25] and the first federal survey on the subject was only undertaken in 1981. In recent years, however, much more information has become available and there is a growing literature on the subject.[26] From the surveys which have been undertaken, a fairly detailed picture of the scope and character of industry's training programmes emerges. First, it is estimated that during 1986 it spent more than thirty billion American dollars on the training of its work force, involving no fewer than 36.5 million employees. Second, as one would expect, the amount of training provided varies both according to the size of the company and the nature of the industrial and business activity. Roughly four out of five companies earmark part of their budget for training, which is much more commonly provided by the larger companies than the smaller ones: as in Japan and the United Kingdom, small concerns find it difficult to finance and provide training facilities. There are also significant disparities between the amount of training provided by different industries: for example, the Federal Government — especially the armed forces — as one of the largest employers of highly skilled and specialised personnel, is among the most intensive trainers, as are the mining industry, transportation and public utiliy companies, and finance, insurance, and real estate. The distributive industry and companies manufacturing non-durable goods, on the other hand, have a relatively poor record of training. Most formal training in indusry is concentrated in the age group from 25 to 44 and is most common among white-collar workers, especially managers, professional and technical workers, and clerical staff. Most employer-based training is undertaken 'in-house', but more than a third is contracted out, principally to vocational training institutions, both public and private. In order to provide the necessary job-specific training, most of the larger and medium-sized companies have established special departments which, like their Japanese counterparts, are increasingly being called, 'human resource development' (HRD) departments. Frequently these departments develop training programmes with the help of outside consultants, and use a wide variety of training methods, including lectures, discussions, discussion groups, films, and slide presentations. A growing concern of many companies is with the retraining of their current work force, due partly to new technological developments and partly to the increased pressure to compete with foreign companies by improving productivity and reducing costs. In a number of states, of which New York is a good example, special programmes have been developed on a statewide basis for this purpose, using community colleges as providers.

During the past six or seven years, technological changes and foreign competition have combined to bring about a considerable increase in the training programmes of most of the larger American companies, particularly among the financial institutions. As a result, a larger proportion of employees in all major job categories is now involved in formal training than was the case in 1980, and company training departments are now better equipped to provide effective training programmes. A particularly interesting development in recent years has been the establishment by a number of large corporations of their own campuses, which now number more than 400.[27] Because of what are said to be deficiencies in the teaching of basic education by the schools, many of these company colleges are offering not only high-level technical programmes, but also remedial courses in basic school subjects. It seems likely that such human resource development, as it is increasingly being called, will grow during the next decade or so, if only because, according to one estimate, three-quarters of all workers currently employed will need retraining by the year 2000.[28]

One of the most striking demographic changes in the American work force since the end of the war has been the dramatic increase in the participation of women. According to Department of Labor statistics they made up approximately 30 per cent of the work force in 1950, whereas by 1982 they accounted for 43 per cent. However, they still remain concentrated in the traditionally female occupational fields and comprise the vast majority of secretaries, nurses and primary school teachers, for example. By contrast, they are very poorly represented in the skilled trades, including those requiring a period of apprenticeship. In recent years, however, efforts have been made to increase the number of women in male-dominated training programmes and jobs, and legislation addressed to facilitating equal opportunities for women and to increasing the number of women in apprenticeship has been enacted by Congress. However, they still constitute only a very small proportion of registered apprentices: in the state of Hawaii, for example, the number of females as compared with the total number of registered apprentices has never been above 6.87 per cent.[29] As we have seen, one of the aims of the Perkins Act is to increase 'sex-equity' in vocational education. Accordingly, it authorised some funds for this purpose and required states to appoint 'Sex Equity Coordinators' to manage them. Since then, some tentative progress has been made in a number of states, but as in many areas accurate information is hard to come by, so that as one writer on the subject puts it, 'Were Congress to ask, today, what the impact of the Perkins Act has been on access, enrollments and outcomes for women and girls, we would be hard pressed to tell them'.[30] Deep-felt attitudes in society at large, the general absence of political will, and the reluctance of the Federal Government, in particular, to devote sufficient funds to improving the vocational training opportunities for women, make it unlikely that the situation will improve much in the foreseeable future.

As far as the *initial training and staff development* of American teachers of vocational education are concerned, as in so many other aspects of the country's educational provision, the picture is a complex and confusing one, with considerable variations from state to state. The position regarding high school teachers of vocational education is succinctly put in the trenchant words of: *The Unfinished Agenda*: 'they tend to be underpaid, underprepared and expected to work miracles'.[31] Unsurprisingly, an increasing number of the best teachers of vocational education are leaving the profession. Moreover, the dramatic drop in the past decade or so in young people completing teacher education programmes — in the early 1970s 21 per cent of all bachelors' degrees were in education, compared to 12 per cent in 1981[32] — has resulted in a shortage of high school vocational education teachers across most of country. One consequence is that in some states, the requirement for newly-appointed teachers of vocational subjects to have completed successfully a course of teacher education is no longer mandatory, and teachers with industrial experience alone are being drafted in and are having to develop pedagogic skills with little or no help. In any case, the entry requirements and quality of initial training courses for vocational education teachers vary considerably from state to state and even from one vocational subject area to another. Some states, such as Hawaii, require intending high school teachers to have a bachelor's degree with specific training in general education, their occupational speciality, and pedagogy, together with work experience. Other states, such as California, recruit teachers with industrial experience, give them a provisional 'licence to teach' and then require them to obtain a 'teaching credential' by attending credit courses provided by the state universities. Yet other states, like Oregon, recruit high school teachers with trade skills, but do not require them to obtain a teaching credential, although they encourage them to do so. Unfortunately, during the past decade the number of would-be teachers undertaking initial training programmes has been steadily and, on occasion, rapidly declining. This is due partly to the relatively low esteem in which teacher education in general, and vocational teacher education in particular, is held within higher education at large, partly because resources for vocational teacher education have been severely eroded, and partly because many school districts in their attempts to save money have been cutting back on vocational education programmes. In order to try to overcome the shortage of vocational education teachers in its schools, Hawaii, for example, has been considering the introduction of an incentive scheme to persuade would-be vocational teachers to train, not unlike that introduced recently in Britain in 'shortage subjects' by the Department of Education and Science. However, the situation is complicated by the fact that there is no standard pattern of initial teacher training which applies to all vocational subject areas. Most states have a number of distinct programmes in such fields as agriculture, business studies, and home economics, which although they are much alike in their requirements, are often offered in separate institutions or departments, so that often neither the trainers nor the trainees in a specific subject area are in regular contact with their counterparts in other vocational areas.[33]

The requirements are just as various for teaching staff in the community colleges and the technical institutes. In California, for example, faculty are required to obtain pedagogic credentials by undertaking a programme, offered by the state universities, which includes courses on such topics as 'Principles and Practices of Vocational Education' and 'Applied Supervisory Processes Relevant to Vocational Education'. Here as in other states, there is a shortage of courses designed for teachers of specifc vocational subjects so that teachers across a range of subjects often have to enrol on broadly vocational programmes, a problem that is also to be found in the United Kingdom and elsewhere. In some states, of which Oregon is an example, there is encouragement for community college teachers to train, but no requirement, so that much depends upon the motivation of the individual and the encouragement or the lack of it which he receives from the head of his department or the dean of his faculty.

If anything, the position regarding the provision of staff development for experienced teachers of vocational education, whether in high schools or community colleges, is even more patchy. In a number of states, teachers are required to be reregistered every five years, and in order to gain a renewed licence to teach they must complete a required number of 'credits' during that time. These 'credits' may be obtained in a variety of ways including long and short courses, periods of employment in industry, and industrial visits and contacts. This system obtains in California, for example, where credit-bearing courses are made available in state universities and are also provided by school districts and various private training agencies. However, the majority of these programmes are theoretical and concerned with pedagogy or management, and there is no requirement in the crucial areas of recent industrial experience and subject up-dating. On the other hand, many Californian community college teachers, for example, obtain up-to-date knowledge of industry and business by working in factories or offices in their summer vacations or part-time during the year, or by being employed by industry as consultants. Moreover, the state Director of Vocational Education is attempting to secure 'credit' for vocational teachers who spend periods of time in industry, a system which, as we have seen, already operates in other states. Inevitably, the range of staff development programmes across the country is both large, and varies greatly in quality. There are, of course, many examples of good practice, usually stemming from the drive and expertise of individuals or groups of dedicated teachers and administrators. One of the states whose vocational education programme is highly regarded across the country is Oklohama, and among its products are training packages, including video materials, which are widely used in staff development programmes at state level. In Oregon, Dr Dan Dunham of Oregon State University has developed a system in conjunction with the state Department of Education, called 'The Oregon Alliance', whose general aim is to improve the provision of vocational education in the state, including the promotion of professional staff development. One of its most interesting aspects is its 'Extern Program' for vocational education teachers wishing to move into middle management: now in its seventeenth year, it aims to develop 'leadership competencies', and to this end uses a range of interesting materials including those developed by the National Center for Research in Vocational Education based at Ohio State University. Similar examples of good practice are to be found in many parts of the country but the overall picture that emerges is inevitably a patchwork quilt of provision. Both in regard to initial teacher training and also subsequent staff development, resources have in many states been severely cut and these will not be restored until and unless state legislators and the public at large are convinced of the value of vocational education and the consequent need to ensure that teachers are properly prepared and that their skills and knowledge are regularly updated and upgraded.

Finally, further reference must be made to the National Center for Research in Vocational Education, which until quite recently was based at Ohio State University in Columbus, Ohio. Over the years, it has built up an enviable reputation, not just for producing commissioned research and influential publications such as *The Unfinished Agenda*, but also for running a wide range of workshops, seminars and conferences, both in Ohio and in various other parts of the country. It also operates no fewer than four data bases containing a vast range of information relating to vocational education. These include the VECM (Vocational Education Curriculum Materials) database, which it runs jointly with six regional curriculum co-ordination centers, and which contains curriculum materials, both printed and non-printed, on all vocational areas; and ERIC (Education Resources Information Center), one of the largest American educational bases which is sponsored by the National Institute of Education. The National Center also has its equivalents at state level and one of the most lively is in the nearby mid-western state of Illinois, the Office of Vocational Education Research directed by Dr Tim Wentling at the University of Illnois at Champaign.

Conclusions

The environment in which America's system of vocational education and training operates has changed greatly in recent years, as in all the other developed countries we have been considering, and will go on doing so. Three major developments which are greatly affecting it are demographic changes, technological developments, and the growth in the 'information economy' accompanied by a decline in a manufacturing.[34] Because of a decline in the birth-rate, the number of potential new workers entering the labour force during the next decade will decrease by about 25 per cent, with considerable consequences for vocational education. With a shortage of trained youngsters entering employment, more emphasis will have to be placed both on increasing the proportion of young people from ethnic minorities who presently take up vocational education, and on persuading girls and women not to restrict themselves to their traditional vocations. The growth in the use of information technology will make it necessary to train many more workers skilled in the use of computers, word processors and similar equipment. Lastly, the increasing rate of technological change will inevitably require a great increase in the provision of updating and retraining programmes for adult workers.

In meeting these challenges, the American system of vocational education and training has certain assets. As we have seen, it is possessed of both flexibility and vitality and allows a great deal of scope for individual initiative. Industry and business are committed to a considerable investment in training, one which has appreciably increased in recent years and looks like going on doing so. The institutions of vocational education and training are able to respond quite quickly to the perceived needs of the labour market, the private training schools more so than the public ones. Moreover, there are many examples of excellent programmes scattered across the country, although the conditions which make them work so effectively are not sufficiently well understood to use them as models elsewhere.[35]

On the other hand, the public sector of vocational education and training, comprising the high schools and the community colleges, has in most states been passing through a difficult period in recent years. Since the Reagan administration came into office in 1981, the financial stake of the federal government in vocational education has proportionately greatly declined. Moreover, many states have placed increasing emphasis on academic excellence at the expense of their vocational programmes, citing Japan as a case in point. In many parts of the country the thrust to raise academic standards in basic school subjects derives from the belief that, in a rapidly changing society, the most effective way of preparing a skilled work force is to impart a sound general education upon which to build later the necessary specific vocational skills, though in this respect, as in so many others, circumstances vary from state to state. In Oklohama, for example, its system of vocational education, or 'Vo-Tech' as it is called locally, is highly regarded and consequently its funds have been less severely cut back than in the great majority of states. In general, however, the United States is moving away from what Grubb[36] terms a 'simple-minded vocationalism' and this is occurring at a time when influential voices in the United Kingdom are citing the supposedly well-developed American system of vocational education as one to be emulated.

However, there can be little doubt that the public institutions of vocational education and training in the United States have an indispensable role to play in training and retraining skilled personnel. Although most large companies are able to provide training facilities for their employees, most small or new businesses are unable to do so, and turn to the community colleges and similiar institutions for help. Similarly, youngsters from disadvantaged backgrounds and women wishing to acquire skills to enter the labour force rely heavily on inexpensive programmes provided by the colleges. Sooner or later it seems inevitable that their historic and current role in training and retraining the nation's work force will be better understood by society at large, and better funded by the Federal and state governments.[37]

Chapter four

The Federal Republic of Germany: A commitment to vocational education and training

The system of vocational education and training in the Federal Republic (West Germany) is one which has attracted a great deal of attention from British observers, and, as a consequence, has been frequently examined by visitors — including politicians, industrialists, civil servants and educationalists — and just as frequently reported on. The reason for our consuming interest in the Federal Republic's provision of vocational education and training is not far to seek: the 'economic miracle' which has led to West Germany raising itself from the rubble of the immediate post-war period to become the most prosperous and economically powerful country in Western Europe must surely, it is said, have something to do with its system of vocational education and training? As the United Kingdom's industrial position and prosperity relative to other developed countries have declined, so that of West Germany have increased. By 1980, for example, as Professor Prais has pointed out,[1] output per employee in manufacturing was some 50 per cent higher in West Germany than the United Kingdom and real income per head of the total population was about a third higher. At the same time West Germany boasts a much more comprehensive and seemingly effective system of vocational education and training, so that it is natural to assume that the former state of affairs derives, in part at least, from the latter.

The Federal Republic of Germany is, of course, a creation of the decade after the Second World War. It grew out of a fusion of the three zones occupied by the American, British, and French armies of occupation and became a sovereign independent country on 5 May 1955. With the exception of West Berlin, which is an outlier embedded in East Germany, its territory is contiguous and is made up of 11 *Länder*, or states: Baden-Wurttemberg, Bavaria, Berlin, Bremen, Hamburg, Hessen, Lower Saxony, North Rhine-Westphalia, Rhineland-Palatinate, Saarland, and Schleswig-Holstein. It occupies an area of almost 250,000 square kilometres and has a population of just over sixty-one million, of whom 49 per cent are Protestants and 44.5 per cent Roman Catholics. Over four million foreigners are living in the Federal Republic at present, of whom almost half come from Turkey and most of the rest from southern Europe. The size of the population within each *Land* varies considerably, from about 700,000 in Bremen to some seventeen million, or more than a quarter of the country's total population, in North-Rhine Westphalia. Its economy is predominantly an industrial one, based on coal-mining, iron and steel, machine construction, electrical and metal products, and the processing of foodstuffs.

The social and educational background

The Federal Republic today is a stable democracy with a federal constitution which lays down the division of power and responsibility between the Federal Government in Bonn and the administrations within the eleven *Länder*. Thus, the federal constitution bestows upon the latter 'cultural sovereignty' which, as far as education is concerned, gives them primary responsibility for the provision of primary and secondary schooling, with the partial exception of vocational education. Indeed, it was not until the late 1960s that a Federal Ministry of Education and Science was established. This system of government represents little change from the past as West Germany has never had a centralised and uniform education system. However, it is important to understand that each *Länd* has a highly centralised power structure which applies to education equally with other aspects of provincial government.

In general, West Germany is both an ordered and orderly society in which most aspects of economic life and educational provision are determined by detailed laws.[2] It has developed a tradition of 'consensus politics' which is based, among other things, on middle-of-the-road Federal Governments, and an elaborate body of constitutional law enforced by a powerful judiciary on both the executive and the legislative.[3] In this context there is general agreement about the importance of vocational education and training, which has long been regarded as an integral part of West German life, and about the parts to be played in its provision by the Federal and *Länder* governments, by employers, by trade unions, and by the individuals themselves. Education is highly regarded and is seen by many as the principal means of bettering themselves.

The school system, which is relatively simple (see Figure 4.1), has, to British eyes, a somewhat old-fashioned appearance as, at lower secondary level, selective schools are predominant and comprehensive schools the exception rather than the rule. Although there are slight differences in organisation and structure between the individual *Länder*, the basic school system is broadly similar across the country, being dvided into three stages: primary, lower secondary, and upper secondary. There are nine years of compulsory full-time schooling from 6 to 15 in most

Länder, with ten years in a few. In addition as we shall see, all West German pupils have some form of compulsory education or training up to the age of 18. Moreover, the compulsory period of schooling is preceded for more than three-quarters of the pre-school population by attendance at *Kindergarten*, whose numbers have grown very considerably in the past twenty years. The primary school, or *Grundschule*, comprises Grades 1 to 4, ages 6 to 10 years, everywhere except in West Berlin and Bremen where it covers Grades 1 to 6, that is from 6 to 12 years. Like primary schools elsewhere, those in West Germany have not been without their problems. These include the procedures for selection for the different types of secondary school which in the past have often been very rigid, bringing pressures upon children and teachers similar to those associated with the formerly widespread 'eleven-plus' examination in the United Kingdom. However, in recent years the transition to secondary schools has become more flexible with the introduction in the first two years of lower secondary school of what are variously described as 'probationary', 'observation', or 'orientation' stages (*Orientierungsstufe*). Their function is to leave open the decision about what the pupil will do next until the end of the sixth grade and then reach this decision on a reliable form of assessment.[4] In many parts of the country, primary schools have had to accommodate substantial numbers of children of foreign workers, *Gastarbeiter*, and many of them have been less than successful in providing multicultural and bilingual programmes for these children.[5]

Once youngsters have completed their four years of primary school, they move on to three types of selective secondary schools: the *Hauptschule*, roughly equivalent to the British secondary modern school; the *Realschule*, or intermediate school, and the *Gymnasium*, or grammar school. The *Hauptschule*, which caters for about 45 per cent of the 10- to 15 or 16-year-old age group, is a five- or six-year school which takes those children who are unable to obtain places in the other types of schools. It has been in decline for some years and inevitably finds itself, especially in the urban areas, with the most backward and most deprived West German children, including a high proportion of the children of the *Gastarbeiter*. Numerous attempts have been made by the *Länder* to revive the *Hauptschule*, for example, by means of curriculum reform and by the introduction of a school-leaving qualification which is recognised as equivalent to the *Realschule* diploma, but these have not been very successful.

On the other hand, the *Realschule*, which now caters for over 20 per cent of the age group, has expanded its position over the past twenty years as an alternative selective institution to the *Gymnasium*. It offers a four-year programme, from age 12 to 16, and its increased popularity is due partly to the fact that its curriculum, emphasising science,

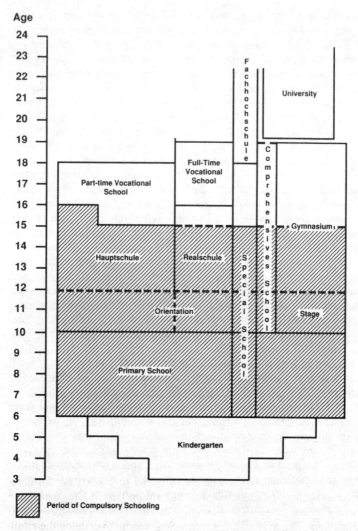

Figure 4.1 The educational system in the Federal Republic of Germany

mathematics and modern languages, is increasingly popular with pupils and parents who see it as a good preparation for later employment or higher education; and partly because the educational opportunities for those completing the *Realschule* have greatly increased. It has proved particularly attractive to children of working-class parents who are deterred by the more elite aura of the *Gymnasium* and who prefer the more practical curriculum available in the *Realschule*.[6]

The *Gymnasium*, which caters for about one-quarter of the age-group, is a nine-year school, from age 10 to 19. It has changed dramatically in the past twenty years or so, both in the social composition of its students and in the curriculum which it offers. Its main function has been, and remains, to prepare students for entry into higher education, principally via the *Arbitur*, the graduation certificate which entitles the school-leaver to study at university. In the past twenty-five years the proportion of school-leavers with the *Arbitur* has grown very considerably, from about 5 per cent to 22 per cent, though a significant proportion of those who are successful nowadays prefer not to enter higher education but rather opt for vocational training courses. Moreover, the changing nature of the *Gymnasium* in recent years means that it is no longer as highly selective as it once was; indeed in some suburban areas it enrols as much as 50 per cent of the age cohort. Increasing numbers of its students, instead of staying on to 18 or 19 to complete the *Arbitur*, leave at 16 in order to attend a full-time vocational school or to start an apprenticeship within the *Dual System*. In this respect their career aspirations are very similar to youngsters leaving the *Realschule*. Finally, the *Gymnasium*, like the other schools, will increasingly be affected by demographic factors, namely the steep fall in the school population which is currently affecting West Germany. In North Rhine-Westphalia, for example, its most populous state, the school population fell from 3.4 million in 1975 to 2.7 million in 1985.[7]

Finally, in a few of the *Länder* there are comprehensive schools, *Gesamtschulen*, which cater only for about 3 per cent of the school population, compared to over 90 per cent in the United Kingdom. Their geographical distribution is very uneven and they are mostly concentrated in the politically less conservative states, namely those with Social Democratic governments, such as West Berlin, Bremen, Hamburg, Hesse and North Rhine-Westphalia. The reasons their supporters put forward for their introduction are similar to those in the United Kingdom: that they are a means of providing equality of educational opportunity for all youngsters, that they enable more young people to develop their full potential, and that they promote co-operation and citizenship among all strata of society. However, their introduction has aroused considerable controversy and has been held up by legal and other impediments. Moreover, even in areas where there are comprehensive schools, a Land must provide the other three types of secondary school in order to ensure that parents have a full choice; this frequently results in the 'creaming off' of the most able students into the *Gymnasium*.

In addition to the four types of public secondary schools described above, there is also a variety of Special Schools which cater, for instance, for physically or mentally handicapped children. These schools accommodate about 5 per cent of the age group. In addition, there is a relatively small private sector of education.

Before examining the provision of vocational education and training which becomes available for youngsters after age 15 or 16, it is important to consider how far their school-leaving attainments provide a sound basis for this subsequent training. In this regard the acquisition of mathematical ability is clearly significant, and it seems indisputable that West German standards are higher than those in the United Kingdom, and that youngsters leaving all the four types of secondary schools have a greater mathematical capability than their equivalents in the United Kingdom. Moreover, about 90 per cent of all school-leavers obtain a school-leaving certificate appropriate to each type of school, requiring minimum attainments in core subjects such as mathematics, science, German and a foreign language. As a consequence, it can reasonably be concluded that the 'schooling stage' in West Germany provides a better foundation for later vocational training than its British counterpart. It also offers a broader curriculum and significantly higher levels of attainment in core subjects, for a greater proportion of pupils;[8]

West German schools also provide more pre-vocational instruction than do their British counterparts, in the form of programmes known as *Arbeitslehre*, or Education for Work, which have been introduced into schools in all parts of the Federal Republic. However, they have been confined to the *Hauptschule* and *Gesamtschule*, and in practice are largely restricted to children of working-class parents. They are essentially pre-vocational in character in that, although they include a period of work experience, they are not designed to provide job-specific training.[9] Their official aims are ambitious and include the provision of a general vocational education to enable youngsters to find an adequate profession, the promotion of vocational and professional flexibility, and making young people aware both of the nature of employment and also of their role in the home and in society at large.[10] *Arbeitslehre* replaces former subjects such as woodwork, metal-work and needlework; however, the precise form which it takes varies from one Land to another. Unlike many school subjects, it is not tied to one related area of learning, but may be taught through several, such as engineering, economics, social sciences and home economics. In this respect, it bears some resemblance to the Technical and Vocational Education Initiative (TVEI) programmes which have been introduced into British schools in recent years. However, the latter are designed for youngsters aged between 14 to 18 of all abilities, while *Arbeitslehre* is provided for the 13 to 16 age range, very largely for the lower half of the ability range.

Arbeitslehre has been particularly well developed in West Berlin where compulsory education continues to the age of 16, and it comprises a general course in such subjects as basic work techniques, typewriting, the reading of technical drawings, consumer information, bank accounts and family budgets; a choice of options from among mechanical technology, electronics, textiles, and household subjects; and career guidance, including talks by local personnel officers and visits to local places of employment. Elsewhere, where compulsory schooling ends at 15, *Arbeitslehre* may be obligatory only for the last three years and somewhat less time may be devoted to it than is the practice in West Berlin.

Inevitably, the introduction and evolution of *Arbeitslehre* have not been without their problems, including the difficulty of organising the programmes over a range of school subjects and ensuring that teachers have the attitudes and knowledge to teach them effectively; and the administrative complications of organising work placements in factories and businesses. While properly organised programmes of *Arbeitslehre*, tailored to the needs of individual students, have much to offer them — for example, in improving their motivation in mathematics and other school subject areas — they do require a high degree of co-operation between those concerned and hinge upon the difficult task of properly integrating the various components of the programmes. Moreover. to work effectively they require special methods of instruction including projects, and the production of goods for sale and even services in the form of repairs and information, which in turn require specific teaching techniques from the teachers concerned and the provision of specialised classrooms. Clearly, therefore, the implementation of effective programmes of *Arbeitslehre* will require more money than traditional school subjects. As they are patronised very largely by lower ability children in the *Hauptschule*, it remains to be seen how much public support they will command.

The provision of vocational education and training

In the Federal Republic, the vocational education and training of youngsters to produce skilled workers takes place once they have completed their general education at school. Thus, for the majority who leave school at 15 or 16, two types of vocational training are available. The first is the celebrated *Dual System* which most youngsters of this age embark upon, whereby as apprentices they combine on-the-job-training in industry or business with part-time, compulsory attendance at vocational schools until the age of 18, and the second consists of attendance at full-time vocational schools, which have been growing in popularity in recent years.

The much admired *Dual System* is the classic way by which the majority of West German school-leavers enter into a vocational training programme. It is characterised by two major features which distinguish it from most vocational training systems in other countries, such as the United Kingdom. First, as we have seen, training is split between two instructing parties: the employer and the school. For one or two days a week they attend state vocational schools (*Berufsschulen*), where they combine general education with the theoretical underpinning of their vocational subject, and for the rest of their working week they acquire practical skills at their place of work. Second, as is apparent from the foregoing description, vocational training takes place to a considerably greater extent in the workplace than in school.

This system of apprenticeship, not unlike that in the United Kingdom which combines workplace experience with day-release to the further education college, though of course in a much smaller and less systematic scale than in West Germany, has very deep historical roots going back to the guilds and the master-apprentice relationships of the Middle Ages. It depends for its success on the willing co-operation of four major parties: the Federal Government, the *Länder* governments, the employers, and the trade unions.

At present, about two-thirds of all young people in the 15 to 18 age group participate in the *Dual System*, which overall caters for about 1,800,000 trainees. During the course of 1986, for example, over 700,000 new trainees were accepted as apprentices, 40 per cent of them girls, in no fewer than 500,000 training firms, approved for this purpose by the Federal Government. These youngsters were training for some 430 different trades in 13 broad categories, although they were largely concentrated in relatively few of them. Moreover, sexual segregation occurs so that the boys especially patronised 'male trades' such as motor mechanics, electricians, machine fitters, joiners, masons, painters, gas and water fitters, salesmen, bakers and locksmiths. These 10 trades accounted for no fewer than 39 per cent of all apprentices.[11] In the case of girls, the concentration in a few trades is even greater, with 58 per cent of all female trainees following one of seven trades: hairdressers, saleswomen, office work, business women, doctor's or dentist's assistants, bank clerks, and retail shop assistants.

The specific training programmes which apprentices undergo are usually of between three and three-and-a-half years' duration, though a large number of occupations require only two years of training, and in some individual occupations training can be completed after one year.[12] In addition, young people with above average school-leaving qualifications, and judged to be of superior learning ability, can have their training period shortened. Subject to the successful passing of examinations, training programmes culminate in qualifications as skilled or white-collar workers. The training which takes place in the employers' premises, which as we have seen comprises the greater part, is governed by a series of federal laws and regulations. Among the most important are the Vocational Training Act of 1969 which specifies the basic legal conditions for the provision of on-the-job training, and the Vocational Training Promotion Act of 1981 which governs the planning of vocational training and the work of the Federal Institute of Vocational Training (the *Bundesinstitut für Berufsbildung* or BIBB), which is part of Federal Ministry of Education and Science, and which, in collaboration with representatives of industry, business and the trade unions, determines what skills and knowledge are required for each occupation. Thus, the BIBB's role is a key one in the *Dual System* in that, among other things, it provides a kind of 'clearing house' in which the various partners in the system — including the *Länder*, the employers and the trade unions — can hammer out agreements on vocational training matters. A very important part in the system is also played by private sector autonomous bodies known as Chambers of Industry and Commerce, Crafts, Agriculture, and certain professions, consisting of representatives of employers, employees and vocational school teachers. The chambers (*Kammern*) are 'responsible agencies' for vocational training and are autonomous, regional organisations to which all firms must belong. The most important chambers are the sixty-nine of industry and commerce and the forty-two of craft. They are responsible, at the end of the apprenticeship, for testing centrally both the vocational elements of the curriculum which are learned largely on the firm's premises, and also those general theoretical aspects learned in the vocational school which are of specific application to the apprenticeship concerned.[13]

The curriculum which apprentices undertake consists of an initial period of broadly-based training lasting about a year, followed by specialist training appropriate to their place of work. Regulations governing curricula for specific trades are agreed upon by the major parties concerned and these are revised and brought up-to-date from time to time. They always include written and practical tests and, often, oral tests as well. A form of quality control derives from the fact that most chambers obtain standard examination papers from semi-commercial bodies set up for this purpose.[14] The awards given by individual chambers are recognised nationally and are valid throughout the country.

The bulk of the costs of training within the *Dual System* are borne by the firms with whom trainees sign a contract which guarantees them employee status. These costs include those of providing instructors, training workshops, machines and materials, and the remuneration of the trainees. In 1985, for example, industry and business spent approximately 20 billion DM on this training. In recent years the amount of money spent by firms on vocational training has risen considerably. This is due partly to the increase in the number of trainees, partly to the need to provide more and better trained instructors and for trainees to spend longer periods in workshops, and partly because an increasing number of small firms are having to send their apprentices to interplant training centres. Both the Federal and the *Länder* governments have also been spending more money in an effort to persuade industry to provide more training places, especially for young people who are disadvantaged in some way, and to improve the quality of vocational training itself. In 1984, for example, they spent more than one-and-a-quarter billion DM on special programmes for pupils at vocational schools, while the Federal Institute of Labour spent over 3.7 billion DM on promoting vocational training on an individual and institutional basis.

As apprentices spend the great majority of their time on the job, it is their employers who largely determine what they learn and where and when they learn it. The firms are concerned both to ensure that their apprentices develop the skills and work attitudes that they consider desirable, and also that the training costs are kept to a minimum. To these ends, they largely limit the skills training to what they consider essential for the occupations in question.[15] However, in order to provide a broader base of vocational training and to delay young people's career decisions, a basic vocational year (*Berufsgrundbildungsjahr*, BGJ) was introduced in the early 1970s. It takes place in the full-time vocational school (see p. 106) and provides knowledge of a broad occupational field from which young people can choose to enter a job-specific apprenticeship. It is intended to be an alternative to the first year of apprenticeship training in a firm and, therefore, to be credited by employers. However, many of them have refused to recognise the BGJ for this purpose, precisely on the grounds that it does not provide job-specific training. As a consequence, the number of young people attending the BGJ has not grown as rapidly as planned, and many young people have enrolled on it because they failed to obtain an apprenticeship place with a firm. With relatively high youth unemployment, their numbers have continued to be quite substantial — in 1986 there were about 93,000 of them — and BGJ has become a 'waiting room' for school-leavers without an apprenticeship contract.[16] Indeed, even after they have completed the BGJ, only about half of the youngsters find an apprenticeship place, and many conceal their BGJ from their employer or receive no credit for it as the first year of their apprenticeship.

The 500,000 firms which provide the bulk of the training under the *Dual System* are to be found across every branch of the West German economy, including industry and business, the service sectors, agriculture, the civil service, professions such as doctors, lawyers and chemists, and in domestic economy. Not all firms provide vocational training, however, and the largest number who do so is in the craft sector where about half of all the training firms are to be found. Moreover, almost two-thirds of the apprentices are to be found in firms with fewer than fifty employees, especially in the crafts, in business, in agriculture and in the professions. As the training programmes approved by the BIIB have to be comprehensive in nature, and as in recent years many smaller firms have become specialised and technical in their operations, so they have found it increasingly difficult to meet the training requirements. While many large companies had solved this problem by setting up their own training schools, where their employees receive the bulk of their in-plant training, because of the expense involved this solution was not available to the smaller firms. However, many smaller firms have responded to this difficulty by coming together to offer co-operative programmes whereby apprentices undertake different parts of their training schedules in different firms. This is an attractive solution in that it involves very few additional training costs, and as new technologies are introduced, requiring more and different training, so these types of co-operative ventures are likely to increase. In addition, numbers of training centres have been established by the chambers or by a guild to which small firms can send their apprentices learning various trades. As these interplant training centres, as they are called, require a high level of investment, the Federal and *Länder* governments have provided them with considerable financial subsidies. Indeed, the Federal Government plans to increase the number of places at the interplant - training centres to a total of more than 77,000.

Within the craft sector, which numerically provides the largest number of apprentices, and where the proportion of trainees to the work-force as a whole is relatively high, the *Meister*, or Master Craftsman, plays a very important role, though his equivalent is also to be found in industry and business. He both acts as a trainer in many instances, and also as an example of status and achievement to which the young apprentice can aspire. The ambitious apprentice can aim to achieve this highly-qualified position by completing his apprenticeship, obtaining industrial experience and further training, and passing appropriate examinations. The role of the *Meister*, both in training, and in industry generally, is so important that it has been described as 'the engine of the German training and industrial system'.

Within the *Dual System*, the part-time vocational schools, the *Berufsschulen*, are the junior partners, as is all too apparent from the limited amount of time trainees spend in them, and from the fact that school achievement records do not count towards the final apprenticeship examination. Their functions are to continue the apprentices' general education and to provide a theoretical complement to their on-the-job training. Attendance at a part-time vocational school is mandatory for the entire duration of the apprentices' training, and they must attend the equivalent of one day week until they turn 19, unless they have already fulfilled vocational school requirements by attendance at a full-time vocational school. During their day at part-time vocational school, trainees devote 60 per cent of their time to vocational training and 40 per cent to general education. In many cases trainees, instead of attending one or two days a week, do so in blocks of several weeks, on a similar basis to the 'block release' of apprentices in the United Kingdom. As in this country, these instructional blocks are designed to allow for more continuous learning and to provide larger interrelated learning units. However, many firms, especially the smaller ones, are reluctant to release their apprentices for these periods as their services are needed at their place of work. It is not surprising, therefore, that many of the same tensions between the partners in training are to be found in West Germany as frequently exist in the United Kingdom between the employers and the further education colleges. Some West German employees complain that the schools do not impart sufficiently job-specific instruction, and it is partly for this reason that many large firms have set up their own in-house programmes of theoretical vocational training within their training departments, to which they send their employees instead of to the *Berufsschulen*. [18] One result of this development is that the latter have become less significant and well regarded, and increasingly cater for trainees from small and medium-sized firms who, not having their own training schools, have to rely on them.

For an increasing number of youngsters the alternative to entering directly into an apprenticeship, with its combination of on-the-job training and day release to the part-time vocational school, is attendance at full-time vocational schools, or *Berufsfachschulen*. As these have not developed systematically but have arisen in response to varying demands and pressures, they comprise a collection of schools and programmes whose variety and labyrinthine nomenclature are confusing even to many West Germans.[19] Their function is not so much to provide a substitute for on-the-job training, but rather to prepare for it and deepen it. Consequently, they fall into three broad types: those in which basic vocational training can be obtained, those which offer vocational preparation, and those in which vocational training can be completed. The numbers of these schools have grown considerably in the past decade so that in 1984, for example, they catered for about 550,000 students, of whom the great majority, or some 430,000, were in schools offering basic vocational training. As we have seen, their courses are usually of one year's duration, which are limited to a prescribed vocational field and which include some general education in the form of German, social studies and physical education. They are open to all young people who have completed their nine years of compulsory education and legally confer partial credit towards the completion of the trainee's requirements providing he or she enters a job within the same occupational area. As a consequence, firms offering apprenticeships must count this basic vocational training as part of the term of the apprenticeship, a practice which has aroused considerable opposition from some employers.

The full-time schools for basic vocational preparation also offer courses of about one-year's duration, which prepare students either to take up regular vocational training or to enter the labour market as unskilled workers. As this type of training conveys basic knowledge and skills which are not job specific, it does not count towards a subsequent vocational training programme.

The third type of full-time vocational school comprises those in which complete vocational training can be obtained, and their courses may be of two or three years' duration. These include schools which train for occupations for which on-the-job training is absent or scarce, such as the health and child care occupations, kindergarten and nursery teachers, business administration, and clerical occupations. Some of these schools require previous practical experience as a condition of entrance, while others provide integrated periods of practical work in their curricula.[20] There are also full-time vocational schools which prepare students for the examination of the various trade associations.

In addition, there are well over a hundred full-time vocational institutions known as Polytechnics, or *Fachhochschulen*. These offer three-year courses in such subject areas as engineering, business management, social work, and design. As, however, they are institutions of higher education, they are outside the terms of reference of this book.

The distribution of the full-time vocational schools, like that of apprenticeships, varies considerably from one part of the country to another, being particularly sparse in rural areas where, understandably, they exist only in such occupations as agriculture and crafts and where, as a consequence, industrial training opportunities are few and far between. By contrast, the large cities offer a wide variety of full-time vocational schools comprising training across virtually the whole occupational spectrum.

Given the nature of the courses offered by many of the *Berufsfachschulen*, it is hardly surprising that over two-thirds of their students are girls. Moreover, as the final certificates acquired at the schools are not usually accepted as a full qualification for blue- or white-collar workers, so a substantial proportion of their students go on to complete a vocational training course in the *Dual System*. The growth in the popularity of the full-time vocational schools over the past decade, together with a trend for youngsters to stay on longer at regular school, have resulted in an increasing proportion of young people entering on-the-job training at a somewhat later age than has hitherto been the case: in the mid-1970s the average age of entrants was 16, whereas by 1984 about a third of them were 18 years or older. As a result, there is no doubt that trainees in general are better educated today than they were, say, a decade or two ago.

As in virtually all the other countries described in this book, West Germany faces acute problems in finding sufficient and suitable training places in the *Dual System* for girls and women, and for the children of foreign workers. As a result, girls and women often find difficulty in finding a training place of any kind and, in 1984, for example, of those youngsters who were unable to do so, almost two-thirds of them were young women. This was because firms tend to give preference to applications from young men, despite the fact that young women generally have higher scholastic qualifications. Industries are often reluctant to offer them training places in what are generally regarded as 'male occupations' and the young women themselves prefer to train for the 'typically female' occupations such as office and sales jobs, service industries, and the care and welfare professions. The Federal Government has made efforts in recent years to open up the trade and technical professions to young women by, for example, offering girls some 1,200 training places on an experimental basis in the electrotechnology and metal-work trades. Experience so far has shown that girls have experienced no major problems in either training or employment in these fields, and it is to be hoped that more firms can be persuaded to make places of this sort available and that the girls themselves can be persuaded to take them up. Not surprisingly, perhaps, these attempts to counteract sexual stereotyping in vocational training have attracted a great deal of favourable press publicity in West Germany, including pictures of young girls wielding bricklayers' trowels, for example, and one beneficial result seems to be that there has been a considerable increase in recent years in the number of girls training for craft and technical occupations. However, West Germany, like The United Kingdom, has a long way to go before anything like the full range of jobs is open to girls on something like an equal footing with boys. Moreover, even when girls complete their training, they generally find it more difficult to obtain a job than boys, and consequently account for a disproportionate share of unemployed young adults.

Much the same is true, sadly, of the children of foreign workers. Young foreigners in West Germany also labour under considerable disadvantages. Although there are more than 200,000 of them between the ages of 15 and 18 who are obliged by law to attend part-time vocational school, only about half of them actually do so, while only one-quarter, or some 49,000, undertake trade training.[21] One of the main reasons for this is that, as only a small number of them have attended school, either full-time or part-time, they have an inadequate knowledge of the German language, and do not possess a school-leaving certificate. Inevitably, therefore, they are heavily affected by unemployment — in

1983, for example, the unemployment rate among teenage foreigners was 21 per cent, compared with 9 per cent for all young people under 20 years of age — and where they do have jobs they are concentrated in the category of unskilled labourers, working more often than not as assemblers, storage and transportation workers, and in cleaning jobs and in food services.[22]

The Federal and *Länder* governments, together with the other interested parties, are making various efforts to improve the training situation for young foreigners. These include the provision of intensive German language courses, special careers advice, measures aimed at the vocational preparation and social integration of young foreigners, and pilot schemes of training which have been running at training firms since 1980. How effective these measures have been it is difficult to judge, but training opportunities for foreign children may well improve over the next few years, if only because with the declining birth-rate, and the consequent drop in the number of West German applicants for training places, firms are likely to be more ready to take on young foreigners.

During the past twenty years or so a number of changes have been made to the basic structure of the *Dual System* in response to changes in the economy, to increasing unemployment, to the changing attitudes of young people towards vocational training, and to demographic trends.[23] As we have seen, these have included the introduction in the early 1970s of the first year of common basic training and the growth in full-time vocational schools. More recently the system has had to face two fundamental problems. First, technological developments such as the widespread utilisation of microprocessors in the workplace, and the increasing specialisation and automation of production, have made it more and more difficult for many firms to provide systematic and comprehensive on-the-job training.[24] Second, for a variety of reasons the demand for vocational training places has in recent years outstripped the supply (Table 4.1). Undoubtedly West Germany industry and business have made valiant efforts to increase the availability of places, and the growth in numbers from 677,200 in 1979 to 719,000 in 1985 represents a considerable achievement, one which took many percipient observers by surprise. Indeed, largely thanks to expansion of inplant training, the percentage of the working population completing their vocational training, according to a survey carried out by the Federal Institute of Vocational Training and the Institute of Employment Research in Nuremberg, rose from 72 per cent in 1979 to 79 per cent at the beginning of 1986. On the other hand, the demand for places has risen even more steeply, as Table 4.1 illustrates, so that the numbers unable to find places year by year have commensurately increased. This has occurred despite a decline in the 15-to-19-year-old group, which in theory should have eased the problem. However, these figures are rather slippery in that while they give a general order of magnitude they do not necessarily represent an accurate picture of the complex situation which exists in many parts of the country. For example, there are inevitably some regions where industry is poorly represented and where consequently youngsters cannot obtain an apprenticeship of their choice. In that case they may turn by default to other trades, or to other measures such as attendance at a full-time course in a vocational school. Moreover, it is the contention of the trade unions, for example, that many young people who are unable to find a training place of their choice become disheartened and no longer apply. In addition, because of the relative shortage of jobs, youngsters who in the past would have sought employment as unskilled workers are now undertaking vocational training to improve their chances of employment; and the growth of unemployment among university graduates has prompted many young people leaving the *Gymnasium* at 18 or 19, especially girls, to undertake trade courses rather than enter higher education.

Table 4.1 Federal Republic of Germany: Availability of training places for young persons, 1979–85

	Available training places	Demand for training places	Availability surplus(+) or demand surplus(−)	Applicants still without training places
1979	677,200	660,000	+17,200	19,700
1980	694,600	667,300	+27,300	17,300
1981	643,000	628,000	+15,000	22,000
1982	651,000	665,500	−15,500	34,000
1983	696,000	724,000	−28,000	47,400
1984	727,000	764,000	−39,000	58,400
1985	719,000	756,000	−37,000	58,900

(Source: Survey, Federal Institute of Labour, cited in 'Learning for the Working World', *Bildung and Wissenschaft*, 1986, p. 25)

However, in the near future there should be first a gradual and then a rapid decline in the demand for training places, with the level in the mid-1990s being about 40 per cent below its peak in the mid-1980s.[25] For the present, however, as unemployment has increased in West Germany during the past decade, so more and more young people have failed to obtain jobs after completing their training periods and, as a consequence, there has been a steep increase in unemployment among 20-to-25-year-olds. As a result of these developments, the *Dual System* is having to cater for rather different types of trainees than in the past, trainees who are both somewhat older and better qualified than their predecessors. Nowadays, as we have seen, about one-third of all trainees are adults, that is, over the age of 18, so that the training they receive, and the methods by which they are taught, should reflect their greater maturity. Secondly, whereas in the past the vast majority of trainees have come from the *Hauptschule*, an increasing proportion now possess either a *Realschule* or *Gymnasium* school-leaving certificate. As a consequence, more and more of them prefer white-collar jobs and make different demands on the training content and methods of their programmes, and on the qualifications required of instructors and vocational school teachers.

In the Federal Republic, as elsewhere in the developed world, the need for the *further vocational training* of the work-force, consequent upon developments in science and technology and the rapid pace of change, has grown apace. Unlike initial vocational training, however, further vocational training is not basically regulated by the state; indeed by comparison it constitutes 'a peripheral area of indefinite shape.'[26] To some extent this works to its advantage, in that a wide range of organisations and types of programme have stepped into the breach, without too much let or hindrance from either the Federal or *Länder* governments. Thus, as one might expect, the main providers are the firms themselves, catering for just under half of all participants. But, in addition, many other agencies are involved, including trade unions and professional associations, the Chambers of Industry and Commerce and the like, and a wide range of private training institutions. These have increased in number in response to the growing demand, so that between 1979 and 1982, for example, the percentage of the work force aged between 19 and 65 who participated in some form of further training increased from 10 to 12 per cent, comprising a total of 4 million people.[27] Unsurprisingly, the bulk of further training is undertaken by skilled and highly-qualified persons, with the unskilled and semi-skilled, women and foreign workers, being poorly represented. The nature of the further training that is provided by the employers, who as we have seen are the major suppliers, is much as one would expect. Over a third of the courses are concerned with new technologies, while data processing and information technology, management training, commercial skills, and industrial and technical skills make up the content of the bulk of the remaining two-thirds.[28] However, these further training activities are largely dependent on the amount of money industry is able and willing to devote to them and only partly reflects the actual need for them.[29] As in the United Kingdom, many of the leading West German companies are much concerned to expand their provision of further training, some of which is not directly related to their workplace skills but consists rather of 'self development' programmes. The reason that these companies are prepared to invest in this form of further education is that, like their equivalent in Japan, they see the need for a better educated and more flexible workforce.

As the need for further vocational training has become pressing, so inevitably the Federal Government has begun to take a greater interest in it. At one time it had intended to transform the area of further training into a full-scale public training system, analogous to the *Dual System*, and to this end in 1968 and 1969 passed two important pieces of legislation: the Employment Promotion Act and the Vocational Training Act. They were designed to provide a legal framework for further training, to lay down standards for determining what forms the provision should take, and provide funding opportunities for employees to attend courses. However, these objectives were never fully achieved as the pressures of growing unemployment, and the unfavourable economic climate, diverted government attention elsewhere. Nevertheless, some Federal Government funds have been made available for this purpose: according to figures provided by West German industry, in 1985 it spent about 10 million Deutschmarks (at the early 1988 rate of exchange, the pound sterling was worth about 3 DM) on further training, while the government provided 5 billion under the auspices of the Employment Promotion Act. The Federal Institute of Labour has been particularly active in commissioning vocational training measures from all the leading providers of training in the Federal Republic, especially for those who are unemployed. In 1986, for example, it promoted over 530,000 people in continuing training, an increase of 30 per cent over the previous year, two-thirds of whom had previously been unemployed, some of them for a long period.

Early in 1988, the Federal Education Minister, Jurgen Möllemann, announced that concerted action was needed by all the interested parties to develop a 'grand consensus' on the need to invest more money in further training. However, he made it clear that the state should not intervene on a large scale, that as much provision as possible should remain the responsibility of the present providers, and that it should continue to be financed by the firms and by the charging of fees. Without an infusion of government funds, it seems unlikely that substantially more provision will be made for those groups presently poorly represented in further training, namely the unskilled and semi-skilled, and the disadvantaged.

Clearly, much of the success both of the *Dual System* and also of further vocational training, depends upon the quality of the training which is delivered, which in turn depends upon a sufficient supply of well-trained instructors. *The training of vocational instructors* is, therefore, taken seriously within the Federal Republic and, in order for a firm to qualify to provide approved training, it must have sufficient qualified instructors. The first qualification requirements of this kind were introduced in 1972, and since then they have been extended to more and more subject areas. Broadly speaking, instructors are required to pass an examination in order to be qualified to train apprentices, an examination which tests their knowledge of the content of basic vocational training, of the planning and execution of training programmes for young persons, and of the legal aspects of vocational training.[30] Instructors, who must be at least 24 years of age, are themselves expected to have personal experience of industry and business. Indeed, instructors are often senior craftsmen or the qualified owners of small shops. Moreover, as the examination for *meisters* in the crafts area has long required instructional ability in addition to technical skills, so all master craftsmen are entitled to train apprentices. In all, there are an estimated 50,000 full-time and between 300,000 and 400,000 part-time instructors in the Federal Republic. As the importance of the role of trainers has become more evident, both to the government and to industry, so their status has grown and, especially in large firms, the post of instructor is increasingly regarded as one which leads to professional advancement.

Conclusions

As we have seen, the main agency of vocational education and training in the Federal Republic of Germany has long been, and still remains, the *Dual System*. Despite frequent prognostications of gloom, of forecasts of impending disintegration under pressure from within and without, the edifice remains substantially in place and in reasonably good working order. Undoubtedly one of its abiding strengths is that within a national and regional framework it remains essentially a local affair embedded in the local community. Moreover, despite trenchant criticisms from time to time from the partners in the enterprise, notably the employers' organisations and the trade unions, it has largely retained their commitment to it. One of its great virtues is that for very many school-leavers in West Germany it provides a smooth transition from school to work. It has also proved reasonably adaptable to changing circumstances and has, for example, accommodated such developments as the introduction of the first-year basic training in vocational school, the *Berufsgrundbildungsjahr*, the increase in the number of full-time vocational schools, and the growth of inter-plant training centres. The demographic changes of the last decade, together with youth unemployment, have led to a greater demand for training places, a challenge which industry has responded to positively, with encouragement from the Federal Government. However, a major cause for concern is that an increasing number of the firms involved in vocational training view their trainees as a form of cheap labour; indeed, in order to make it easier for firms to provide extra training places, the Federal Government has to an extent relaxed the conditions governing entry qualifications and the like, thereby increasing the likelihood that some firms will exploit their trainees.[31] Moreover, the expansion in the number of training places in recent years is bringing about the production of substantial numbers of skilled workers for whom demand may well decline over the next few years. This is particularly true of those occupations in which female workers predominate, so that the average length of vocational on-the-job training for women is less than that for men. Doubtless this is because many firms are only interested in hiring them for a limited period of time, and are therefore reluctant to invest much time and money in training them. To a large extent the same circumstances hold true for the children of foreign workers and, as we have seen, both groups suffer disproportionately from unemployment when compared with men of German origin.

Nevertheless, for the great majority of its trainees, the *Dual System* appears to deliver a form of vocational training which is of a high quality. In addition, the extent of the system is such that vocational qualifications are much more widespread in West Germany than in the United kingdom: Prais and Wagner[32] estimate, for example, that some 60 per cent of the West German labour force have obtained apprenticeship or similar vocational qualifications by examination, compared with 30 per cent at the most in the United Kindom. The result of this system is the training of a high quality labour force which clearly has much to do with the high quality products for which West Germany is world famous. Certainly the Federal Government itself appears to have little doubt on the subject, as the following quotation from an official publication amply testifies,

> The acknowledged quality of German products, the irrepressible lustre of 'Made in Germany', the persistent competitive power of the German economy world-wide — all these factors are attributed by observers of German development not least to the high level of qualification and large number of German skilled blue collar and white collar workers. Both are the result of vocational training which enjoys an important place in the education system.[33]

However, the stresses and strains on the *Dual System* are likely to increase into the foreseeable future, with the need to adapt itself to rapidly changing technology, and to promote among its trainees creativity and the ability to innovate. Equally important is the need for West Germany to make more provision for the retraining and further training of young people aged between 20 and 25 years, a group which has been disproportionately affected by unemployment. Indeed, rapid changes in technology with accompanying effects on industrial organisation and production, while not invalidating the principles upon which initial vocational training as enshrined in the *Dual System* are based, make it more and more essential that highly developed countries like West Germany invest more heavily in recurrent and further training. The indications are that, having adapted itself to numerous changes in the past, the West German system of vocational education and training will successfully face up to this challenge, too.

Chapter five

The United Kingdom:
A Reluctant Revolution?

The United Kingdom of Great Britain and Northern Ireland is at one and the same time a relatively wealthy country, the majority of whose people enjoy a high standard of living as measured by most criteria, and yet one whose relative position in terms of its international standing and its industrial and commercial competitiveness has, until quite recently, steadily declined since the end of the Second World War.[1] A small and densely populated country, it occupies an area of just over 244,000 square kilometres, about the size of the American state of Oregon, with a population of approximately 56 million, of whom about 2.5 million are from ethnic minorities, of New Commonwealth or Pakistani origin.

Consisting of England, Scotland, Wales and Northern Ireland, each of which has its own special features, but all of which have much in common, the United Kingdom is a constitutional monarchy and a parliamentary democracy. Its constitution is partly unwritten and its basic sources are Acts of Parliament and decisions made by courts of law, many of which have in recent years concerned its provision of vocational education and training. Since the end of the Second World War it has had to come to terms with a traumatic retreat from Empire and has increasingly turned instead to its continental neighbours, culminating in its joining the European Economic Community at the beginning of 1973.

The social and educational background

The United Kingdom's decline as a leading international power, both politically and economically, can be traced back many decades. However, its most obvious manifestations, including the shedding of its empire, are relatively recent. Compared to its major industrial competitors such as the United States, Japan and West Germany, its position deteriorated more or less continuously during the past forty years, and only during the past year or two has the trend shown signs of reversing. Using such basic criteria as economic growth, the rate of inflation, the state of the balance of payments and the level of unemployment, the United Kingdom fared worse than all the major countries which are her competitors and principal trading partners. The reason for this unhappy state of affairs are many and complex and were ascribed, a little simplistically perhaps, by the Conservative Government, in its 1985 White Paper, *Employment Policy*, to a combination of managerial inadequacies, union obstructionism, excessive government regulation and the discouragement of the entrepreneur,[2]matters which it is attempting to set right. This concern with the country's faltering economy has led the present government, like some of its predecessors, to foster a national system of vocational education and training, perceiving a close link between an effective training system and an efficient economy. Compared to some of our industrial competitors like Japan and West Germany, the United Kingdom has traditionally eschewed any firm government policy in this area and instead relied upon industry and business, together with some discreet governmental pressure, to provide training for its own employees. However, by the 1960s it had become quite apparent that this voluntary system was not working very well, and that industry required more stimulus and incentive to provide training on a national scale. The upshot was the passing of the 1964 Industrial Training Act, which provided for the establishment of twenty-three statutory industrial training boards (ITBs) for industries which together employed about half of the country's work force. The ITBs were charged with the responsibilitiy of ensuring an adequate supply of trained men and women at all levels of industry, and with improving the efficiency of training. However, within less than twenty years they were perceived by their political masters to have largely failed in these endeavours with the result that by 1983 all but seven of them were closed down, the major ones that remain being those for the engineering and construction industries. In the meantime, the ITBs had come under the control of the Manpower Services Commission (MSC) which was established by the government in 1974, and whose principal aim is to promote economic growth by developing the country's manpower resources and by promoting skilled training. Since then, it has grown greatly in influence and powers and has introduced a number of training initiatives, including the 1983 Youth Training Scheme, which will be discussed later in the chapter.

In the past twenty years or so since the passing of the Industrial Training Act, the United Kingdom has witnessed several major developments, each of which has considerable implications both for its economy and also for its training system. The first of them was the steep decline in the birth-rate which occurred some twenty years ago and has since levelled out. Thus, the number of live births fell from about 830,000 in 1967 to approximately 600,000 in 1975, with the result that the number of young people entering the labour market is currently declining and will go down steeply over the next few years. Second, the nature of the

British economy, like that in Australia, for example, has undergone a sea change. During the last two decades the most notable trend in employment has been the decline in manufacturing and the growth in the service industries, notably distribution, insurance, banking, professional services and public administration.[3] Accompanying this shift in the pattern of employment has been a steady increase in the percentage of women employed in the labour force. Third, and sadly, the last decade or so witnessed a steep rise in unemployment; in 1970, for example, the unemployment rate was about 500,000, whereas by 1986 it was just over three million. Since then, however, there has been a steady, and continuing improvement in the situation, so that by March 1988 the jobless total was just over two-and-a-half million, or 9.1 per cent of the working population, thereby bringing the United Kingdom's unemployment rate below that of Belgium, France and the Netherlands. This steady drop in unemployment is attributed partly to economic growth, and partly to the large number of young people on training schemes. Indeed, one of the very worrying features of the past decade has been the high level of youth unemployment which, in some parts of the country, and especially among young people from ethnic minorities, has probably approached 50 per cent of young people seeking employment. If the present improvement in the productivity and competitiveness of British industry is to be maintained, it will require a steady supply of skilled personnel and this in turn will depend on effective training schemes being widely available both for young people and unemployed adults.

As far as educational provision in the United Kingdom is concerned, it has developed separately in England and Wales, Scotland, and Northern Ireland respectively, so that there are in effect three separate systems. However, as all three have a great deal in common, and as that in England and Wales is by far the largest and the one with which I am most familiar, it is that one upon which this chapter will concentrate. As space precludes a detailed description of the education system in England and Wales, upon which there is in any case an extensive literature,[4] only its major features will be dealt with here. Its overriding characteristic and tradition has been one of devolution, whereby responsibility for the provision of education lies with local government, in the shape of 105 local education authorities in England and Wales, while the central authority, the Department of Education and Science, formerly the Ministry of Education, oversees the system. Thus, in the 'maintained', or public, sector, attended by the vast majority of young people, schools and colleges are run by the local education authorities, who also employ the teachers and determine the curricula, though much of the responsibility for the latter is left in the hands of the teachers themselves. However, if, as seems likely, a major new education bill shortly passes through parliament, this situation will radically alter, with, for example, the introduction of a

National Curriculum and the opportunity for schools and further education colleges to 'opt-out' of local authority control. In the meantime,
the present method of operation can be characterised as a national
framework, locally administered. Reflecting this partnership, the education system is financed roughly equally by funds provided by the central
government through what is called the Rate Support Grant (RSG), and
funds raised locally by the local education authorities through the 'rates',
essentially a form of local property tax. In recent years, however, concern
about the quality and character of the education provided by the
maintained sector has led the government to adopt a more dirigiste policy,
culminating in the new Education Bill. This policy has taken a variety
of forms, such as the earmarking of a proportion of the Rate Support
Grant for specific educational purposes, and the placing of the control
of part of the funding of the further education colleges in the hands of
the Manpower Services Commission — the latter development will be
examined in more detail later.

The present structure of educational institutions (Figures 5.1) derives
from the 1944 Education Act, together with subsequent amendments,
which established a consecutive system, divided into three sectors:
primary, secondary, and further. Children attend primary schools from
5 to 11, and secondary schools from 11 to 16. At age 16, they may stay
on in full-time education in schools until 18 or transfer to a further education college for the same purpose; in either case, the education remains
free. One variant on this arrangement, adopted by some local authorities,
is to introduce a third tier, known as the 'middle school', whereby
children attend primary schools from 5 to 8 or 9, middle schools from
8 to 12, or 9 to 13, and secondary schools thereafter. In the Western
European tradition, post-war secondary schools in the United Kingdom
developed along selective lines, with academic 'grammar' schools for
what were deemed to be the academically able, and 'modern' schools
for the majority of youngsters. However, in the past 30 years or so,
these selective schools have very largely given way to comprehensive
secondary schools which, along the lines of the American high school,
recruit from virtually the whole ability range. Although the precise form
which the comprehensive schools take, in terms of the age range for
which they cater, varies from place to place, they now predominate
throughout the country and are attended by more than 90 per cent of
the secondary school population. Alongside the maintained school system,
there is also a small but influential private sector catering for about 7
per cent of the secondary school age group, of which the best known
institutions are the so-called 'public schools', though in paradoxical
British fashion they are not public, but private.

The curriculum provided by the British schools is much like that in
comparable school systems throughout the world, and consists of a broad

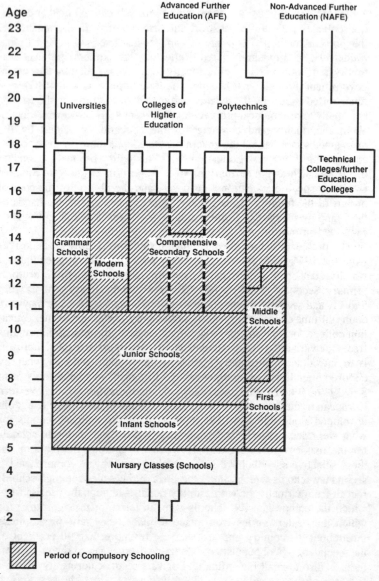

Figure 5.1 The educational system in the United Kingdom

range of subjects, which, however, narrow down dramatically to a relatively few specialist subjects in the post-compulsory period of schooling from 16 to 18. The curriculum is essentially an academic one, though in recent years the government has been attempting to nudge it in a broadly vocational direction by such means as the Technical and Vocational Education Initiative (TVEI), a pilot scheme designed to introduce children to vocational studies in the secondary school and to provide a bridge with the world of work. As we have seen, the government proposes to introduce a National Curriculum with particular emphasis being placed on the 'core' subjects of English, Mathematics, and Science. However, with very few exceptions, British secondary schools, unlike American high schools, make virtually no provision for occupational specific programmes.

It is at age 16 that, like its Australian counterpart, the British system moves away from those in Japan and the United States where the great majority remain on at school until age 18. Here only a small proportion do so: in England and Wales, in 1983, for example, less than 18 per cent of the 16-19 age group stayed on at school. The options open to the great majority of 16-year-olds leaving school after the period of compulsory education are essentially three-fold: they may enter a college of further education to undertake full-time study for either vocational or general qualifications; they may enter full-time employment, with or wthout part-time study at the further education colleges; or they may be unemployed, in which case the great majority of them will enter the two-year Youth Training Scheme for unemployed school-leavers. For those undertaking academic courses, whether in secondary schools or futher education colleges, the standard programme is the one which leads at age 18 to the General Certificate of Education (GCE) Advanced Level which is, in effect, the key to entry into higher education.

At this stage, it is necessary to clarify the very confusing terms 'further' and 'higher' education, which in typical British pragmatic fashion overlap and blur one into the other. Broadly speaking, the further education sector consists of all post-secondary institutions, other than universities. These comprise colleges of further education (including technical colleges and specialist institutions such as colleges and institutes of agriculture and of art), polytechnics, and colleges and institutes of higher education. The colleges of further education, or technical colleges as they are sometimes called, very largely offer courses up to and including GCE Advanced Level and its vocational equivalent and these are designated as Non-Advanced Further Education (NAFE), while the polytechnics and colleges and institutes of higher education concentrate on courses beyond GCE Advanced Level which are designated as Advanced Further Education (AFE). Just to make confusion more confounded, however, many of the colleges of further education offer a few AFE courses and many of the polytechnics and colleges of higher education offer a proportion of NAFE courses. Nevertheless, the vast majority of vocational courses at craft and technician level are concentrated in the colleges of further education and it is with these that we shall be largely concerned. The term 'higher education' is taken to mean all courses beyond GCE Advanced Level or its vocational equivalent and, therefore, comprises AFE, offered in polytechnics, colleges and institutes of higher education and some collegs of further education, together with the university sector. In other words, the British further education sector, unlike TAFE in Australia, for example, includes slightly more than half the students taking courses of higher education, and the polytechnics and colleges and institutes of higher education, unlike the Australian Colleges of Advanced Education, are not a separate sector but firmly within further education.[5] Unfortunately, the take up of higher education by British youngsters compares most unfavourably with virtually every other developed country. In 1981, for example, only 19 per cent of 18-year-olds in the United Kingdom were in full-time education and training, compared with about 60 per cent in Japan and the United States. At the other end of the spectrum, the degree of overlap between NAFE and the secondary school sector has steadily grown. As we have seen, the colleges of further education offer academic courses like GCE and the school sector is increasingly involved in pre-vocational programmes like TVEI. The logical institutional extension of this overlap is the introduction of the *tertiary college*, which in many ways is indistinguishable from the average college of further education but differs from it in that, in a given catchment area, it is the only post-secondary institution for the 16 to 18 age range. In other words, the last two years of the secondary school system in such areas have been decapitated and the schools here finish at age 16. This arrangement is proving increasingly attractive to many local education authorities who, because of the steep decline in the age group, find it uneconomic to duplicate GCE courses, for example, in secondary schools and further education colleges. This complex institutional pattern has developed as a result of the prevailing British system of devolution which, until recently at least, has encouraged local authorities to develop forms of provision which they consider most nearly meet local needs and conditions. In this respect it provides a sharp contrast with the much more highly-centralised educational systems in Japan and East Germany.

The provision of vocational education and training

Bearing in mind the complex picture of British educational provision we now turn to a detailed examination of vocational education and training which, at operative, craft and technician level, is provided by the maintained colleges of further education, in the form of Non-Advanced Further Education (NAFE); by the private sector of further education; and by industry itself. However, even as late as the beginning of the present decade, as Corelli Barnett has pointed out,[6] more than half of our 16–year olds were leaving school without a qualification which would be valued by an employer, and only 30 per cent of them were enjoying systematic job preparation or further education before entering the job market. It was scarcely surprising that fewer than half as many British workers in manufacturing industries were annually qualifying as craftsmen compared to West Germany, with its broadly comparable population.

Non-Advanced Further Education has traditionally been the major provider with industry and business, of vocational training,[7] and in the United Kingdom, on 31 August 1984, there were almost 2,230,000 students undertaking courses of non-advanced further education leading to recognised qualifications, either vocational or academic. Of these, 392,000 were studying full-time or on a sandwich course basis, and 1,837,000 part-time, including some Youth Training Scheme trainees undertakng off-the-job training in further education colleges. As the country with the largest population, England has the largest number of NAFE students, and provisional figures for 1986 show there were 1,705,000 students in that year, of whom 322,000 were full-time and sandwich, 1,259,000 part-time, and 124,000 on off-the-job YTS training. The proportions of male and female students vary widely according to the nature of the courses: in construction, engineering, agriculture and science, young men predominate, while in secretarial studies, beauty therapy, hairdressing, fashion, hotel reception, and travel and tourism, female students are much more numerous. For much of the post-war period the conventional pattern of non-advanced further education has been for a substantial proportion of youngsters leaving school and entering employment to be released by their employers on a part-time basis, either through 'day' or 'block' release, in order to undertake a college course leading to a vocational qualification. Many of the young men who acquired skill training in this way did so as part of their apprenticeship programme. In addition, in some areas such as training for employment as secretaries, a predominantly female occupation, and in the catering trade, many youngsters attended, as they still do, pre-employment full-time courses at the futher education colleges. Then, as now, one of the major features of the training courses provided by the colleges is that the qualifications they lead to are awarded by a national system of examining and validating bodies which together help to ensure national standards and a major degree of consistency and comparability of content and level. Among the plethora of such bodies, three stand out as catering for the largest number of trainees wishing to be technicians, craftsmen, or operatives. These are the Business and Technician Education Council

(BTEC) and its Scotish equivalent (SCOTVEC) which were set up by the government to establish a national system of sub-degree courses and qualification, mainly at technician level, for occupations in science, engineering, and business and public administration, among others; the City and Guilds of London Institute (CGLI) which is the biggest single examining body in the country with over 550,000 candidates annually for the examinations it offers across a very wide range of occupations, principally at craft and operative levels; and the Royal Society of Arts which annually examines several hundred thousand candidates through its examinations in the commercial and secretarial fields.

While this system, by which young people in employment can obtain vocational qualifications mainly by part-time study in further education colleges, is still in operation, there have been substantial developments during the past ten years which have radically altered the traditional college role.[8] These developments have resulted from the traumatic changes which have taken place in the British economy during the last decade, together with a series of government initiatives, particularly those associated with the Manpower Services Commission.

As we have seen, this period has witnessed a decline in manufacturing production and in heavy industries such as steelmaking and coal-mining, with the result that the apprenticeship system — essentially a male prerogative — has greatly shrunk. Thus, in 1968 the number of apprentices in manufacturing reached a peak of 236,000, whereas today they are fewer than 100,000. At the same time, the apprentice system itself is in the process of being modernized so that the traditional time serving is being replaced with skill testing systems and new, modular forms of training. The effects on the traditionally important college departments, such as engineering and science, have been profound, as the disappearance of many of their students has caused them to decline. At the same time there has been a greatly increased demand for personnel trained in business and office skills, especially from the public sector, with the result that business studies departments have grown greatly in many colleges. Equally, the caring, leisure and service industries have flourished and the colleges are called upon to train increased numbers of young people for such areas as the health services, tourism and catering. As students and their parents rapidly become aware of the job opportunities in these areas, so for some years now many courses providing relevant qualifications have been considerably over-subscribed. Finally, the introduction of new technologies into industry and business, especially in the areas of automation, robotics and the use of computers, microprocessors and word processors, has also greatly increased the demand upon the colleges for personnel with these particular skills.

Perhaps the single most important change in the work of the colleges during the last ten years has been due to the growing impact of the

Manpower Services Commission (MSC),[9] which in 1988 was renamed the *Training Commission.* Established in 1974, it took over the industrial training boards which sponsored college courses, and the Training Opportunities Scheme (TOPS) initiated in 1972 for retraining redundant workers, which took up many colleges places but which has since declined in scope and been incorporated into a recent MSC initiative to promote adult retraining. In the fourteen years since its establishment, the influence of the MSC over the colleges has greatly increased, so that in many of them as much as 40 per cent of their revenues are derived from MSC-funded programmes. The first major step in this direction came in 1978 with the introduction by the MSC of the Youth Opportunities Programme (YOP) for jobless school-leavers. Although the majority of YOP trainees were placed in industry and business, many also attended the colleges, mainly on a part-time basis. With the rapid rise in youth unemployment, the numbers on YOP greatly increased, and the programme itself was soon subject to heavy criticism both on grounds of lack of quality and also as an inadequate response to social and economic needs.

In response the MSC, deliberating upon the inadequacies of YOP and the need for an effective national system of industrial training, put forward a series of proposals which were incorporated into the government White Paper, *A New Training Initiative: A Programme for Action*, at the end of 1981. It laid down three major objectives: to reform and develop the outmoded system of apprenticeship, to extend adult retraining and skill updating, and to move to a position where all young people under the age of 18 not continuing in full-time education should have the opportunity of entering a period of planned work experience and related training and education. Initiatives to achieve all three objectives have since occurred, each with considerable effects on the colleges of further education, and the last resulted in the replacement in 1983 of the Youth Opportunities Programme by the much more ambitious *Youth Training Scheme* (YTS), a one-year programme of training for all youngsters under the age of 18 not in full-time education, including those who were in employment as well as the unemployed. Soon the one-year YTS programme was also seen to be inadequate, and following the recommendation in the 1985 White Paper, *Education and Training for Young People*, the scheme has now been extended to two years. This latest development has been described as a tacit raising of the school-leaving age to 18.

In its original form YTS set out to introduce youngsters to an occupational area rather than give them job-specific training, though it did include an element of training. In the words of the MSC, YTS is based on eleven 'Occupational Training Families' (OTFs), which reflect the general nature of the training and do not contain elements which are specific to a particular job, or skill, or employers. Each OTF is based upon a common 'key purpose' — for example, in the case of the Personal Services and Sales OTF, the satisfying of the needs of individual customers and for the Transport Services OTF, the movement of goods and people — and has a range of learning objectives which are designed to cover the essential competencies required in a job in any industry and in any sector of the economy. In practice, YTS has developed a concentration of approved training places in four OTFs, so that over three-quarters of them are in Administrative, Clerical and Office Services, Personal Services and Sales, Installation Maintenance and Repair, and Manufacturing and Assembly. This pattern is broadly similar throughout the country and seems likely to remain stable for some years to come.

Under the new two-year model, YTS will retain the broad OTF approach for the first year, but it seems likely that the second year will be more occupationally related and may well lead to qualifications such as those awarded by the CGLI. The scheme, which is funded by the MSC, has been administered by MSC-approved Managing Agents which consist mainly of industrial and business concerns, as well as private training agencies of one sort or another. In addition, MSC itself has acted as a Managing Agent approving training places provided by sponsors such as Community Projects, Training Workshops and a group of 176 Information Technology Centres. The last-named have been set up in the last five years to train school-leavers in computer programming and electronic engineerng, some in the deprived inner city areas, and are funded partly by the MSC and partly from industry and local authority sources. Many of the Managing Agencies have turned to the further education sector to provide off-the-job training courses, and the MSC itself has developed a system of 'linked' courses mainly in the colleges of further education in which the students are college-based and undertake periods of work experience in employers' premises. Consequently, although the majority of YTS trainees receive their work experience and related training in industry and business, a substantial minority attend courses in the colleges. Thus, in each of the first two years of YTS, approximately 300,000 trainees took part in the scheme as a whole, of whom more than a third spent some time in the colleges. According to figures issued by the MSC in its review of YTS in 1986–7, during that year there were 360,000 first time entrants on the scheme, of whom 57 per cent were young men and 43 per cent young women (Table 5.1). According to the MSC, the difference is accounted for by the fact that young women tend to stay on at school longer. Nine out of ten young people entering YTS for the first time in 1986–7 were 16-year-old school-leavers joining YTS with a two-year entitlement, and most of the rest were 17–year-olds with a single year entitlement. Ninety-five per cent of the entrants were white, and most of the others were from ethnic minorities. By the end of October 1987, as the two-year YTS gathered momentum, there were about 431,000 trainees in training of whom some 158,200 were in their second year of training.

Table 5.1 United Kingdom: Youth Training Scheme entrants, 1986-7

Characteristics of entrants	Number of entrants	Percentage of total entrants
16-year-old school leavers	323,100	90
17-year-old school leavers	35,900	10
18 to 21-year-old school leavers (disabled, special needs)	1,000	—
White	342,700	95.2
Black/African/Caribbean descent	6,500	1.8
Indian sub-continent descent	5,400	1.5
Others (including those who preferred not to say)	5,400	1.5
Male	204,500	57
Female	155,500	43
Totals	360,000	100

(Source: MSC, *YTS 86–87: A Review of the First Year of 2 Year YTS*, p. 11)

Of the young people who left YTS in the period from April to September 1986, 61 per cent went into work, about half of them with the employer with whom they had trained, and of the remainder 22 per cent were unemployed, and the rest were doing other things including undertaking further education courses. In various ways, therefore, YTS has had a considerable impact on the further education colleges and it has brought through the college doors a large group of youngsters, many of whom have few, if any, formal academic qualifications, some of them poorly motivated towards further study. The formidable challenge for the colleges is to devise suitable courses that will interest and motivate these youngsters.

Although YTS is clearly a great improvement on its predecessor, YOP, it has not been without its shortcomings, or its critics. For one thing, it has not been taken up by all the young people who are eligible for it, some unemployed youngsters regarding it as inappropriate or unhelpful. Second, as we have seen, the intention is to make it available to all those under 18, including those in employment, but so far relatively few youngsters in work have been released to take part in it. Indeed, it is widely regarded as a form of special provision for the young unemployed rather than as an integrated programme of education and training for all young people, whether in employment or not. Third, a proportion of trainees have not completed the full year of the one-year YTS programme, so that the average length of stay on the scheme during its first few years of operation has been 42 weeks. However, it does not necessarily follow that the premature departure of YTS trainees denotes incomplete training or the waste of resources as it may be the case that in some occupational areas, a training period of nine or ten months is sufficient.[10] Finally, the quality of the programmes has been very variable, inevitably in a national scheme put together in a very short time with a high degree of improvisation, and the successful integration of on-the-job learning and off-the-job training has been a particular problem. On the other hand, a recent survey[11] has found that across the country YTS has improved the quality of training in a number of ways: by sharpening existing training programmes and by widening them to include more skills, by adding new elements of training such as health and safety training, and by promoting extra expenditure on equipment for training. The most beneficial effects of YTS seem to have been felt in certain industries, notably engineering, retailing, hotels and garages.

YTS has substantially increased the number of youths being trained, so that during the first three years of its existence nearly one million young people have passed through the scheme, and nationally about 60 per cent of them have left YTS to enter work or a full-time course of further education or training. Moreover, the range of training programmes provided under YTS has spread across many sectors of employment including some in which, previously, little or no provision was made.[12] A good example is the construction industry where The Construction Industry Training Board, one of the largest of the remaining seven ITBs as well as being the biggest Managing Agent in YTS, has annually been providing 18,000 training places, mostly with its large employers. Under the new two-year YTS model, the Construction ITB ensures that during their second year the vast majority of trainees get employment contracts which entitle them to apprentice rates of pay instead of the standard, very modest, trainee allowance.

Well aware of the deficiencies of a scheme which to a considerable extent are the inevitable results of policies which had to be formulated very quickly in response to urgent needs,[13] the MSC has introduced a number of new measures to improve the standards of the programmes being offered. These were outlined in the 1986 government White Paper *Working Together — Education and Training*: on the clear understanding that YTS should be a permanent feature of vocational education and training in the United Kingdom, it specified that Managing Agents would not be allowed to provide training beyond April 1988 unless they achieved Approved Training Organisation status by satisfying a number of rigorous conditions; a new inspectorate, the Training Standards Advisory Service, has been set up to monitor programmes and to help the spread of information and good practice; and a Youth Certification Board has been established to secure recognition of qualifications obtained through YTS, though its function will be subsumed within the new National Council for Vocational Qualifications (NCVQ) whose role is examined later. In addition, renewed efforts are being made to increase the amount of integration between the on-the-job and off-the-job elements of the programme. Finally, the MSC is anxious to improve equal opportunities within the new two-year YTS, having been criticised by the Trades Union Congress and others on the grounds that it discriminates against ethnic minorities by, for example, keeping young blacks in some parts of the country off training schemes offering the best chance of a permanent job, and that it is guilty of sexual stereotyping by channelling young women into 'traditional' courses such as secretarial subjects and beauty therapy.[14] While contending that access to all training programmes is equally open to either sex, and that part of the blame attaches to the entrenched attitudes of the young girls themselves, and to prejudices among employers, the MSC concedes that much needs to be done and will both require the new Approved Training Organisations to demonstrate a positive commitment to equal opportunity and will also monitor the participation rates of ethnic minorities and young women in all YTS schemes.

While it is still far too early to make a definitive assessment of the effectiveness of YTS, the largest and most substantial of the MSC's training initiatives, clearly the scheme is here to stay, and the MSC itself appears to have emerged as a government-sponsored national training agency, as its recent change of name to the Training Commission clearly indicates. One of the major problems it will have to solve if it is to turn into a national system of vocational education and training for *all* youngsters under 18 not in full-time education is its low status in the eyes of many people who see it as a scheme expressly designed for the less able, the less motivated and, above all, those youngsters who are unable to obtain employment.[15] Even where unemployed youngsters are concerned, as we have seen, many of them leave YTS programmes before they have run their course, and even if they stay on to the end may come out partially trained and without any commitment to further training. It is for this reason that a 1987 House of Commons Report recommended that all YTS trainees should obtain appropriate vocational qualifications before they leave the scheme. In the meantime, the impact of the YTS on the non-advanced sector of further education is considerable and will continue to be so.

Adult retraining, on the other hand, has hitherto taken a back seat compared to youth training, both in respect of government policy and also in its impact on the further education colleges. The major retraining programme for unemployed adults has been the *Training Opportunities Scheme (TOPS)* which, as we have seen, began in 1972 and reached a peak of about 100,000 students in 1978, over half of whom were taking courses in the colleges, the rest being trained in MSC Skillcentres and in company training centres. Since then, the numbers of TOPS trainees have declined considerably and the acronym 'TOPS' has now been subsumed into the relatively recent Job Training Scheme (JTS). Until the last few years, government policy towards adult retraining has been ambivalent, and in some instances positive harmful: because of its insistence on applying commercial criteria to the work of Skillcentres, for example, a number of them were closed down in the early 1980s. However, as we have seen, the 1981 White Paper, *A New Training Initiative: A Programme for Action*, included as one of its principal aims the extension of adult retraining and skill updating, and since then a number of initiatives have flowed from both the MSC and the DES. The first of these was *The Open Tech*, launched by the MSC in 1982 for a five-year period.[16] Based to an extent on techniques pioneered by the Open University, during the five years of its existence it largely concentrated on the creation of learning material for adults wishing to train as technicians or supervisors. Much of the Open Tech Unit's energies have been devoted to open learning methods, especially in the field of high technology, involving both the use of existing training facilities and the development of software, and a number of further education colleges have been involved both in helping to develop suitable software and in making their facilities available to adult students. As a result, an increasing number of adult trainees are making use of 'flexi-study' systems developed by a number of colleges which enable them to combine study at home with access to college tutorial help and facilities. Recently, the Open Tech has been replaced by an Open Learning Branch at the MSC.

A much more ambitious MSC-funded initiative in the field of Open Learning is the recently established *Open College* which has stated its intention of aiming eventually to reach millions of students on an individual basis through government programmes like the Job Training Scheme, or through companies. If that should come about, then the Open College logo will become a very familiar part of our system of vocational education and training. The principal purpose of this potentially huge training initiative is to provide a means whereby employees can update their skills or retrain at their own individual pace. In the meantime, the first courses began in September 1987 and the administrative structure to make this possible has taken shape. A national network of about 100 'Gateway' or 'Open Access' Centres has been established, usually based in existing colleges of further education centres, at which students can enrol and, on payment of a fee, obtain study packages and tutorial help, supplemented by television broadcasts. For those students who prefer to undertake courses by correspondence, the Open College has established a National Distance Learning Centre, based at the Open University at

Milton Keynes, which eventually should be able to handle 10,000 students. In addition, broadcast material will be made available through one of the major television channels and by local radio. The courses will operate at various levels, culminating in qualifications awarded by the major examining and validating bodies such as the City and Guilds, the Business and Technician Education Council, and the Royal Society of Arts. A good deal of interest in Open College courses has been expressed by employers and it is likely that a proportion of its students will be undertaking tailor-made courses for particular companies. Although the courses are intended primarily for those in employment, they are also likely to be taken up by unemployed people with the help of financial subsidies. The first 40 or so courses which began in September 1987 include the basic skills of numeracy and literacy; service industries such as travel and tourism; manufacturing industries, including electronics, computer-aided design and manufacture, and robotics; business and office skills; and support of those engaged in organising and teaching programmes of vocational education and training in industry and through YTS. Clearly, if the Open College, which is required to be self-financing by 1991, should prove successful in attracting large numbers of students, then it will involve a major contribution from many further education colleges.

However, the first auguries have not been very promising as, towards the end of 1987, the Open College was facing serious recruitment problems. It is hoping to enrol some 50,000 students by September 1988, the end of its first year of its existence, but it seems that initial recruitment has been much lower than was hoped for. Among the possible reasons for the relatively low take-up of Open College courses may be the relatively high cost of courses and problems in distributing prospectuses and other materials.

The Open College forms part of what has come to be called the MSC's Adult Training Strategy, another aspect of which is the provision of MSC-funded courses along traditional lines specifically for adults. As a result, most colleges have developed both full-time and 21-hours a week courses for adults, some of them supported by the European Social Fund of the European Economic Community, in such areas as construction, hairdressing, catering, commerce and high technology.

Finally, the MSC introduced its *Job Training Scheme* (JTS) in April 1987, a training programme for young adults between the ages of 18 and 25 who have been unemployed for some time. Although still in its infancy and operating on the basis of a pilot programme, JTS rapidly became controversial and ran into resistance, both from trade unions and a number of labour-controlled local authorities who accused the government of using it to introduce cheap labour and depress wages. Moreover, unemployed people themselves have not been attracted by the scheme. As a consequence, instead of the 230,000 adult unemployed whom it was hoped would enrol on JTS programmes, only 37,000 had attended them in the first six months of its operation. Moreover, about a quarter of them had literacy and numeracy problems and many had no formal qualifications at all. In addition, some employers, especially among the larger companies, have been reluctant to take on JTS trainees and the quality of training provided by the smaller companies has left something to be desired. As a result, the government announced towards the end of 1987 that JTS will be replaced by a new programme, to be introduced in September 1988, which will embrace anybody from 18 to retirement age who has been out of work for more than six months, and will provide them with some on-the-job training and, if necessary, further education. It is hoped to provide places for 600,000 people, in the first instance; however, it remains to be seen if the new scheme will work any more effectively than its predecessor.

In addition to the MSC, the Department of Education and Science has also involved itself in two initiatives designed to promote vocational education and training, known by their acronyms PICKUP and REPLAN. PICKUP or Professional, Industrial and Commercial Updating to give it its full title, is a systematic attempt to foster the design by educational institutions, including some colleges of further education, of short updating courses specifically for industrial needs. Its main features include persuading institutions to ensure that their courses meet the particular needs of industry, as perceived by industry itself; that they market their courses effectively; that they are taught by staff both knowledgeable in subject matter and also adept at teaching young adults; and that the courses are offered at an economic price. Although this may all seem a tall order and although PICKUP was launched by the DES, in May 1982 with very limited financial backing, its achievements to date are impressive. Although accurate figures of the numbers of students taking the short courses are not available, Twining[17] estimates that by 1985 the annual throughput was of the order of 500,000.

The second initiative, the REPLAN programme, is funded primarily by the Department of Education and Science and the Welsh Office, with a minor contribution from the MSC. Set up 1984 and intended to continue at least until the end of 1989, REPLAN is designed to bring about more and better educational opportunities for adults who are out of work. Its main elements include programmes of development projects, of which there are over eighty to date, managed by the National Institute of Adult Continuation Education (NIACE) and the Further Education Unit (see p. 136); an associated programme involving local education authorities and their colleges in carrying out projects for the planning, co-ordination and development of education for the unemployed; and the creation of special learning packs by the Open University. The precise form which the projects take varies from local authority to local authority; for example, they include a scheme in one city whereby the unemployed set up their own community workshops, college courses of skills training in different parts of the country, and the exploration of new ways of publicising opportunities for vocational education and training for unemployed adults. REPLAN operates only in England and Wales, there being no parallel programmes in Scotland, and in the former countries at least there is reason to believe that it has enriched the education scene.[18]

Whether these various initiatives, by the MSC and the DES, constitute a co-ordinated national strategy for providing adult retraining and updating is open to question, and in many ways they give the impression of a range of shots fired at the target with more or less success. However, the MSC, in particular, is devoting more and more of its attention to adult retraining, and is currently undertaking a major review of the situation. As we have seen, further education colleges are already much involved in this field and will become more so in the next few years. Thus, the proportion of the funds obtained by the colleges from MSC-funded programmes will grow as will the influence of the MSC over their work.

This influence was greatly increased by another government initiative, announced in the February 1984 White Paper, *Training for Jobs*, whereby 25 per cent of the money allocated for what is called 'Work-Related Non-Advanced Further Education', or WRNAFE, to add yet another acronym to the many which proliferate throughout vocational education and training, would be made available to local education colleges through the MSC. 'WRNAFE' is a portmanteau term for the bread-and-butter technical and vocational courses offered by the colleges, and the new funding arrangements have operated since the financial year 1985–6. In order to qualify for these funds, the colleges are required by the MSC to submit for approval both a detailed 'development plan' covering three academic years, and also one-year 'programmes of courses' of WRNAFE. The object of the exercise is to give the MSC sufficient leverage over the colleges to ensure that, in part at least, they offer courses which, in the view of the MSC, meet national needs for skilled personnel. As we have seen, the MSC also funds the largely school-based Technical and Vocational Education Initiative (TVEI); as a proportion of youngsters on TVEI, usually aged 16 and above, attend further education colleges for part of the programme, so it too contributes to the financial stake which MSC has in their work. As the Manpower Services Commission is part of the Department of Employment, which is also responsible for allocating the Rate Support Grant to local education authorities, it is with accuracy that a recent DES publication describes 'the five-way split of responsibility' in NAFE as resting between itself, the local education authorities, the Department of Employment, the MSC, and industry and business.[19] Indeed, in some educational quarters, both in the institutions and among the local education authorities, there is growing concern that government policy seeks to remove vocational education and training from the local authority sector and lodge it with the Manpower Services Commission.[20]

Although the further education colleges have always had close links with industry and business, these have had to be strengthened in recent years; in order to survive many colleges have had to adopt a much more entrepreneurial policy than was previously the case, and seek out customers in their immediate commercial and industrial environments. As a result, colleges increasingly offer local industry and business tailor-made courses, usually of a fairly short duration and designed to meet specific needs often involving the updating of equipment or processes.[21] Industry frequently asks for these kinds of short courses, some of them based on distance learning procedures, and also calls upon the colleges to provide consultancy services.

In the process of responding to the needs of local industry and business and to the requirement of national bodies like the DES and the MSC, the colleges have had to become more 'accountable'. This increase in accountability has been accompanied by a much higher level of reporting, monitoring and evaluation. In 1985, for example, the Audit Commission of the Department of the Environment issued a report, *Obtaining Better Value from Further Education*, describing the ways in which resources are utilised in the colleges and suggesting improvements. This has resulted in several initiatives to assess the cost efficiency of the colleges, such as the establishment of a joint DES-local authority study group on the subject, and the adoption by some colleges and their local authorities of the Further Education Management Information System (FEMIS), a computer-assisted system designed by the Further Education Staff College (see p. 138) to monitor the cost effectiveness of the colleges.

Finally, in many ways the greatest changes in the colleges, both in organisation and in teaching and learning methodologies, have stemmed from some of the major curriculum developments which have taken place in recent years.[22] Among them have been the introduction of new BTEC courses which have progressively involved college teaching staff in the devising of syllabuses, including many who have previously had little or no experience of it; the introduction of programmes of vocational preparation such as the Youth Training Scheme and the Certificate of Pre-Vocational Education (CPVE), the latter being a one-year, full-time course, provided by schools as well as further education colleges, to introduce 16-year-olds to a broad occupational area while at the same time continuing their general education; and the adoption of new approaches to teaching and learning involving Distance and

Open Learning and more flexible modes of study. The provision of courses for the 16 to 19 age group, whether pre-vocational like the CPVE, job specific, or academic like the General Certificate of Education and the new General Certificate of Secondary Education, is so varied and confusing that they have accurately been described as 'a jungle'.[23] Within the area of job specific or 'traditional vocational' courses, the qualifications that are available from some 250 examining and validating bodies are legion, and as a result students often find difficulty in progressng from one level to the next. This has led to repeated demands for a more coherent approach to the education and training of the 16 to 19 age group[24] and, in particular, for a review of the whole structure of vocational qualifications. Although in Scotland the Scottish Education Department launched its 'Action Plan', a new 'modular' framework for non-advanced technical and vocational education in 1983, until recently little that is comparable was attempted in England and Wales. However, in 1986 the government finally followed suit, albeit on a much broader basis, by establishing the *National Council for Vocational Qualifications (NCVQ)*, to which it has given the remit of devising a national framework of vocational qualifications to be fully implemented by 1991. This framework should be more easily understood than the present confusion, by employers, students and their parents. The NCVQ is an accrediting and not an examining body and is currently formulating the criteria by which major organisations such as BTEC, City and Guilds and the Royal Society of Arts must abide if they are to receive the Council's endorsement of their awards.

To date, NCVQ has adopted a structure of four levels of awards, ranging from courses which impart basic skills to those which operate at 'higher technician' level, and is considering a fifth one. It is proposing a system whereby trainees can accumulate 'credits' leading to awards, not just by successfully completing conventional college courses, but also through work-based learning experience, attendance at short courses, and by open learning programmes. Moreover, in order to obtain these 'credits', it is proposed that trainees should demonstrate what is called 'occupational competence' based on a combination of skills, knowledge and the ability to apply them in the work place; however, the identification and assessment of 'occupational competence' is not likely to be an easy matter.[25] The advantages that NCVQ see for this approach are that employers will be able to identify much more easily than at present the level of skill possessed by an employee or an applicant for a job, and that skill-updating will also be easier as existing qualifications will relate to specific levels of competence on which individuals can build. On the other hand, fears are being expressed within the further education sector and by influential bodies such as BTEC and the Further Education Unit that NCVQ has bowed to the wishes of the employers and the MSC by taking too narrow and job specific an attitude towards training, and that broad vocational education will suffer in the process. At the time of writing this important debate is in its early stages and it remains to be seen how it will be resolved. In the meantime, the Council has launched a pilot project for some specific training areas with a view to national implementation towards the end of 1989.

Several references have already been made to the activities of the *Further Education Unit (FEU)*. Set up in January 1977 by the DES as the Further Education Curriculum Review and Development Unit, its functions, as its original title indicates, are to act as a focal point for curricular matters in further education, and to promote a more co-ordinated and cohesive approach to further education development in England and Wales. During the ten years of its existence it has concentrated on research into curricula for the 16 to 19 age group, particularly relating to the interface between education and work and, more recently on further education staff development. On these, and indeed other subjects, it has published a great many documents and sponsored many research projects, and in a variety of ways has made a substantial impact upon non-advanced further education. In the last few years, sadly its annual budget has been severely cut back, a retrograde step at a time when its work makes an important contribution to the further education service as a whole. As we have seen, the colleges providing non-advanced further education have been subjected to unprecedented changes during the past decade or so. Major changes in curricula and teaching methods; the decline of the apprenticeship system and introduction of different types of students into the colleges on MSC-funded courses; innovations in learning techniques such as distance learning, flexistudy and computer-assisted learning; and rapid technological developments requiring regular and frequent updating, have all continued to bring intense pressure on further education teaching and administration staff. As a consequence, the need for a national and effective system of *teacher education and staff development* has never been greater. In a typically pragmatic British fashion, the response has been *ad hoc* and patchy. With the exception of Northern Ireland, there is no requirement in the United Kingdom for further education teachers to have successfully completed a recognised course of initial teacher training, with the result that little more than half the full-time staff teaching courses of non-advanced further education have done so. However, in recent years there has been a steady and commendable increase in courses of initial teacher training validated by the Council for National Academic Awards, the autonomous body which awards degrees and other qualifications to students undertaking courses in further education institutions. These are provided mainly on a regional, in-service basis at further education teacher training centres (FETTCs), comprising polytechnics and colleges of higher education in association with local further education colleges in England, and University College, Cardiff, usually in collaboration with the appropriate Regional Advisory Councils (RACs), bodies which have the responsibility for co-ordinating further education provision in different areas of England and Wales. However, the total number of teachers trained in this way still represents only a small proportion of those who remain untrained. In addition, there are several other initial training programmes which, although not recognised by the DES for purposes of official qualification, are often of considerable value to the participants. Among the most important ones are the City and Guilds Further Education Teachers' Certificate (730) which has at present some 7,000 entrants, many of them part-time teachers; and a range of teachers' qualifications, mainly in office skills, offered by the Royal Society of Arts. Overall, however, no systematic and far-reaching national provision of teacher training for further education staff is possible without the infusion of resources by the government and this is extremely unlikely to happen in the foreseeable future.

However, an example of the way in which such a development can take place is offered by Northern Ireland.[26] In the province, unlike the rest of the United Kingdom, education is almost totally funded by the Department of Education, Northern Ireland (DENI), which therefore can and does impose a strong, centralised control. In 1983 DENI decided, for a variety of reasons, to introduce mandatory teacher-training for all new entrants to further education colleges. This mandatory programme consists of a one-year day release induction course; however, it also provides for those who wish to do so to proceed further and qualify for a Certificate in Education validated by the University of Ulster, either directly after the completion of the Induction Programme or within a period of three years. Very significantly, to date over 95 per cent of the Induction students have chosen to progress to the Certificate in Education. Moreover, the introduction of the mandatory requirement for new further education teachers has stimulated demand among existing untrained teachers in the colleges who are anxious to obtain a recognised teaching qualification. These encouraging developments carry a strong message for policy-makers in the rest of the United Kingdom.

Equally important for further education staff as initial training are programmes of staff development to improve their pedagogic skills, to improve their managerial capabilities, and to update their subject knowledge. In this respect, too, a patchwork quilt of provision has developed involving, in varying degrees, the Regional Advisory Councils, the local education authorities, the further education teacher training centres, the Further Education Unit, individual further education colleges and a few universities. The recent HMI survey, *NAFE in Practice*, in reviewing thirty-four colleges, concludes that, although staff development takes place in one form or another in every college, it depends on individual initiative and there is rarely an overall college policy for staff development in, for example, the use of more effective teaching and learning methods, or of information technology. The Further Education Unit has also commented on the lack of co-ordination of staff development programmes nationally and on weaknesses in analysing and identifying specific needs, and points to an increasing recognition that it should be 'curriculum-led'.[27] Under new arrangements outlined in a Circular issued in 1986, the DES has placed much of the responsibility for the provision and financing of further education staff development in the hands of the local education authorities, which it says should be responsible for a whole range of national, local and community needs. As a result, a pattern of 'grant-related in-service training', or GRIST, is developing across England and Wales, which is taking a variety of forms in different local authority areas including a wide range of programmes of staff development. However, only modest additional sums of money have been made available for this purpose and it remains to be seen how far an effective long-term and efficient national system of much-needed staff development will result.

Another important organisation concerned with promoting staff development in further education is the *Further Education Staff College*, at Coombe Lodge, Blagdon, near Bristol. Opened in 1963, it provides a venue where, by means of short residential 'study conferences', senior staff and others from the futher education service can meet one another, as well as people from industry and elsewhere, to exchange information, ideas and experience. It regularly issues a series of Conference Reports and these together with the conferences themselves have contributed substantially to the analysis, evaluation and development of the further education system. In recent years, it has published a series of very useful books on such subjects as the management of further education colleges and on education and training in Western Europe.[28]

In any case, it is not just the further education service that is in need of such provision, but all those involved in industrial training, both within and without industry. The Manpower Services Commission has for some time provided short training programmes for the staff of managing agents of YTS through its network of over fifty Accredited Training Centres set up for that purpose. However, attendance at these centres has not been mandatory, and perhaps for that reason has been lower than has been hoped. More recently, however, the MSC has come to realise that the success of the whole of the United Kingdom's system of vocational education and training depends to a large degree on what it calls 'training the trainers'. In a recent discussion document,[29] it estimates that up to a third of the country's work force have some kind of responsibility for staff development, and sets out a strategy for improving their performance. Among the aims of the proposed strategy are the raising of the level of awareness throughout industry and business of the importance of training to their commercial success, the encouragement of the setting up of criteria for national standards for trainers, and the stimulation of new initiatives in updating and developing trainers. It has begun to move in these directions and has increasingly involved further education colleges and their staffs by, for example, providing courses which train some college staff as training consultants. It is also working with the DES, the Further Education Unit and the Further Education Staff College on specific development projects to help vocational education staff to develop their skills in organising and marketing staff development programmes.

In the foregoing account of the contribution of the non-advanced further education sector to the national system of vocational education and training, some clear threads emerge. First, the nature of the work undertaken by the colleges has changed greatly, particularly in the past decade, as old traditional programmes, like apprenticeships, have withered and new ones, like the Youth Training Scheme, have come in. Second, they have had to adapt to the needs of more than one paymaster for, as we have seen, a substantial proportion of their revenues is now derived from MSC-funded programmes and, as so often is the case, he who pays the piper calls the tune. Moreover, their formerly clear role as colleges responsible to local education authorities looks set to change again, as the government enacts proposals to enable some colleges to 'contract out' of local authority control and operate largely independently, albeit under governing bodies on which industry and business are powerfully represented. While the student body within the colleges has probably remained much the same in total, while changing in character, they now represent a much smaller proportion of the country's provision of vocational education and training than was the case ten years ago. A variety of new training agencies, many private in character, have come upon the scene since then, and it is their role we shall proceed to examine. However, as the recent HMI survey, *NAFE in Practice*, confirms, the further education colleges, despite certain deficiencies, are providing a service which is both flexible and responsive to national and local needs.

The contribution of the *private sector of further education* to the national system of vocational education and training is considerable and largely unrecorded. Consisting of independent establishments which offer to students over the age of 16 full-time or part-time courses broadly comparable to those offered by further education colleges in the maintained sector, the only substantive published account of their activities seems to be that of Williams and Woodhall[30] which was based on research undertaken in 1975. They described the private sector as both diverse and volatile and with great variations in size of institutions, standards, and types of courses. They identified 565 colleges at that time with 466,500 students of whom 52,500 were full-time, 54,000 part-time and 360,000 on correspondence courses. A more recent estimate, however,[31] suggests that there are currently about 1,000 institutions in this sector, with probably more than 100,000 full-time students. The majority of these students, apart from the many overseas students taking courses in English as a Foreign Language, are concentrated in business and secretarial colleges and a large number of specialist colleges for such areas as beauty therapy, cookery, engineering, law and nursing. As with private colleges in Japan and the United States, British independent further education institutions respond directly to labour market needs and, like their international counterparts, they are relatively expensive and their courses are usually quite short compared to those in the maintained colleges. In the case of beauty therapy, for example, private colleges offer courses leading to a full beauty therapist's diploma in ten months compared to courses usually of two years' duration, leading to similar qualifications in maintained colleges. The difference in duration is partly accounted for by the fact that the latter usually have larger numbers of younger students to whom they have an educational responsibility, so that they require them to attend general studies classes, for example, and partly because holidays are also very much longer in maintained colleges than those in the concentrated private courses which are highly vocationally-orientated. Moreover, for 16- to 18-year-old students, the courses in the local authority colleges are free, whereas private colleges of repute will charge several thousand pounds. On the other hand, the products of the latter usually enter the labour market considerably earlier, as their courses are shorter. Inevitably, the standards of the private institutions are very variable, and as some of them are run by unscrupulous individuals whose sole motive is gain, the quality of their courses sometimes leaves much to be desired. As a result, in some subject areas where there is great demand for places, and fierce competition among colleges, the results have been described as 'sometimes reminiscent of the frontier lands of the American Wild West'.[32]

Until 1982 the Department of Education and Science operated a voluntary scheme of 'recognition as efficient' for independent colleges, and about 100 were so recognised. However, the scheme was withdrawn in order to save manpower, a decision which disappointed the recognised establishments and made it more difficult for students to receive any guarantee of institutional standards. In order to fill the gap, a number of organisations have been established or expanded by some of the colleges to grant recognition and accredition: these include the British Accreditation Council for Independent Further and Higher Education, which was established in 1984, and the Conference for Independent Further Education which was founded in 1973. However, these and similar organisations represent only a minority of the independent colleges.

The private sector has also expanded in direct response to the growth of the Youth Training Scheme. The network of Managing Agents set up under the scheme has been encouraged to buy in off-the-job training programmes, not just from local authority further education colleges but also from private training organisations, some of which are themselves designated as Managing Agents. For example, a 1986 MSC survey of 616 Managing Agents providing Youth Training Scheme programmes in the year 1985–6, revealed that 108, or about 17.5 per cent, were private training companies. Some of them are well-established agencies which have added YTS courses to their existing programmes, while others have evolved in order to take advantage of this lucrative market; in both cases, they can frequently offer training programmes at a lower cost than the maintained colleges. However, the quality, or lack of it, of some of these programmes has aroused considerable criticism in some further education quarters[33] and, indeed, has been a matter of concern to the MSC itself which has recently been closely monitoring the private Managing Agents to determine whether they should be awarded the status of Approved Training Organisations. If present government and MSC policies continue, which seems very likely, then competition between the private sector and the maintained colleges will become fiercer, in which case the style of presentation of their wares may be as important a factor as the quality of the training packages being offered.[34]

Clearly, the importance of the private sector of further education in the national system of vocational education and training is considerable. In 1975, for example, Williams and Woodhall estimated that it enrolled about 13 per cent of all public sector enrolments and about 18 per cent of full-time students, and since then these proportions have almost certainly increased. While the private institutions fulfil an important function in filling gaps in public provision, their considerable variation in standards is, or should be, a matter of concern to the Department of Education and Science.

As in every developed country, the *training provided by industry and business* in the United Kingdom is very significant, though exactly how much there is, and of what quality, it is impossible to say as no accurate statistics are available. In order to fill this gap the Manpower Services Commission is undertaking the first complete survey of training in the United Kingdom, designed to show how much training is being undertaken by employers, by the government, and by the education service. In a preliminary report,[35] it estimated that employers are currently spending about £5 billion on vocational education and training, compared to £7.1 billion by the public services, and £1.3 billion by the Armed Forces. A recent MSC survey of the British labour force shows that only 2.5 million employees, or just over 10 per cent of the country's work force, are currently receiving training, and that this total includes those on the Youth Training Scheme and on various government-sponsored work schemes. By any count, this situation compares unfavourably with the much more comprehensive training programmes provided by employers in Japan, the United States and West Germany, a dismal picture which is corroborated by a number of recently published reports and surveys on the subject. The 1984 report by Christopher Hayes, *et al.*, *Competence and Competition*, for example, revealed that, on the best evidence, the United Kingdom work force had significantly poorer qualifications relevant to employment compared to those of our major competitors. Then, in June 1985, the MSC published *Adult Training in Britain*, the report of a survey carried out for it by IFF Research Ltd into the training attitudes and activities of 500 employers throughout the United Kingdom employing over twenty-five people in all types of private sector business. It revealed that employers invested on average £200 per employee per year on training, comprising a meagre 0.15 per cent of their turnover, and that while the average British employee received fourteen hours a year off-the-job training, his West German counterpart received thirty to forty hours. The report also concluded that while successful businesses had increased their training activities by 25 per cent over the previous five years, 24 per cent of establishments had provided no training of any kind in the past twelve months and 69 per cent of all employees surveyed had had no training. The correlation between training and the economic success of individual businesses appeared to be high: thus, among the top performers, nine out of ten had carried out training involving nearly half their employees, while among the low performers only a little over half had given any training, involving fewer than one in five of their work force. Another, more recent, survey of 104 employers in the Humberside region showed that only 61 per cent of them had any explicit training policy and that this was much more common amng the larger firms who more frequently earmarked specific training budgets.[36]

In November 1985, another influential report appeared, *A Challenge to Complacency*, prepared by Coopers & Lybrand Associates for the Manpower Services Commission and the National Economic Development Office (NEDO). It concluded that few employers thought that training was sufficiently central to their business to be a main component in their corporate strategy; that many of them showed a complacency, a lack of concern, and in some cases a distressing lack of knowledge about their training needs and provision; and that changing this situation would be an uphill task. The reasons for this lamentable state of affairs include the fact that, too often, training was not seen as an important contributor to competitiveness, but rather as an overhead to be minimised; that once having trained their employees they were liable to be 'poached' by other firms; that uncertainties about future markets, prospects and technological developments were a positive disincentive; and that there was little external pressure to invest in training, from their competitors, from employees and unions, and — with the notable exception of the Youth Training Scheme — from the government. In the words of another recent report on management education, too many of the United Kingdom's middle managers are positively antagonistic towards training, and in many companies apathy and ignorance on the subject are widespread.[37] As in the United States, however, the commitment of employers to training varies greatly from industry to industry. Many of our largest companies, especially among the public and utility services, have effective and long-established training programmes; on the other hand, in the distributive trades, for example, while some nationally-known companies are acknowledged leaders in the training field, many remain unaware or unconvinced of the need for training, or lack the resources to carry it out.[38] This lack of resources is a particular problem for small firms who, by their very nature, are designed to respond quickly and flexibly to market changes and often lack well-developed forward plans. As a result, devising suitable training packages for their employees, many of whom tend to be recruited from the relatively young or as part-time labour, primarily female, is particularly difficult.[39]

By comparison with its principal competitors, British industry also suffers from a relatively underskilled work force and from serious skill shortages. According to a survey carried out by the Engineering Industry Training Board,[40] one in five of British engineers and technicians has no qualifications at all, and only one in fifty has a degree or equivalent qualification; and a recent comparison of British and West German firms by the National Institute of Economic and Social Research concluded that the superior training of West German foremen and charge hands was one of the msot significnt differences between the two countries. Moreover, the gap between the United Kindgom and West Germany shows little sign of closing, as the former annually qualifies between twice and three times as many fitters, electricians and building craftsmen as the United Kingdom. As a survey carried out by the North-east Trades Union Studies Information Unit and published in 1987 demonstrates, a steep decline in apprenticeships over recent years has resulted in a serious shortage in that region in skilled craftsmen in the construction industry, especially plumbers and bricklayers. As yet the Youth Training Scheme has not compensated for this shortage, although the new two-year version with its more job-specific content may eventually help to do so. The construction industry throughout the country faces particularly difficult problems as its work force has declined greatly in recent years and, according to the Construction Industry Training Board, only one in ten of its labour force is currently being trained. This is largely due to the fact that the industry is increasingly dominated by small firms, who for various reasons are averse to taking on apprentices. As a result, although the industry is presently expanding, there is a serious shortage of skilled workers, and there are fears that it is already too late to solve the training crisis.[41]

Another very important area in which skill shortages are hampering the United Kingdom's economic development is that of information technology. The use of computers and microelectronic equipment of various sorts is growing so fast in industry and business that the number of skilled personnel required is increasing too rapidly for the maintained further education colleges to meet the needs of the labour market. However, despite cuts in resources, many of them are expanding their computer departments as quickly as possible and some colleges are providing interesting and innovative programmes tailor-made for local industry.[42] To some extent the private colleges have also stepped into the breach, having sprung up or expanded in response to a lucrative market. The government has also taken a number of initiatives and, in 1985 for example, provided an earmarked sum of money for extra initial and conversion courses in computing. However, a serious gap remains: the Policy Studies Institute estimated that in 1985 there was a shortage of engineers and technicians with microelectronics expertise of the order of 21,000 in manufacturing alone, and if the needs of the service industries and business are added, the shortfall must be at least 60,000.[43] One reason for this lies in the difficulty in attracting girls and women on to computer courses, which are still largely seen as a male prerogative. Part of the problem goes back to the schools where, although in theory boys and girls have equal access to computers, intense pressure on equipment has meant that boys tend to get preference, and part of its stems from the conservative attitudes of young women themselves. As a result, girls and women are poorly represented among skilled information technology staff at all levels and, in the engineering industry, for example, a few years ago only 2 per cent of technicians were women.[44] As the spread of information technology increases across all sectors of the economy during the next few years, it is increasingly imperative to ensure that our system of vocational education and training is geared to meet the growing demand for qualified personnel.

A major reason for the skill shortages which are holding back the United Kingdom's industrial development is that, compared with their equivalents in many of other developed countries, our managers are themselves short of skills. As a recent report[45] reveals, only 21 per cent of top British managers have degrees or professional qualifications of any kind, while 36 per cent of middle managers have had no management training at all since they started work. One result is that too often they fail to recognise the need of training, for themselves as much as for their employees. As this situation is the product of many years of neglect, even with the best will in the world it will not easily be put right.

As we have seen, a major development in vocational education and training was the abolition a few years ago of the majority of the Industrial Training Boards (ITBs), which in some quarters is regarded as having had a seriously adverse effect on provision. Of the original 23 ITBs, only seven are now left: the largest are those for the Engineering and Construction industries, and the other five are for Clothing and Allied Products, Hotel and Catering, Offshore Petroleum, Plastics Processing, and Road Transport. In addition, there is the Agricultural Training Board which is responsible to the Ministry of Agriculture. In order to replace the vanished ITBs, some 120 voluntary training associations have been established which have been operating with varying degrees of success. One of the most lively bodies of this kind is the British Printing Industries Federation Training Organisation (BPIF) which was set up in 1982 and which, since then, has made a significant impact on training in the industry, especially in the reform of apprenticeship training. In addition to developing high quality updating programmes for workers in the industry, it has introduced a new apprenticeship scheme which replaces the former time-serving approach with one that is based on trainees achieving standards of competence. Another forward-looking industry has been hairdressing which has also, in some parts of the country, provided alternatives to the traditional appenticeships. In West Sussex, for example, a consortium of employers was set up in April 1983 as an MSC Managing Agency and, in collaboration with local colleges of further education, training is shared between the colleges and a number of 'non-LEA centres' consisting of hairdressing salons run by employers. One indication of the growing recognition by industry of the need, not just for training, but also for updating and keeping the work force in touch with advancing technology, has been a considerable increase in the number of candidates for the 'Skills Tests' operated by the City and Guilds. These programmes of retraining which impart well-designed, specific skills were taken by 50,000 candidates in 1985, compared to 39,000 in 1984. On the other hand there are still too many industries and employers where the 'non-statutory' organisations have been much less effective.

Conclusion

There is undoubtedly a widespread acceptance in the United Kingdom that, by comparison with other leading nations, our system of vocational education and training is inadequate and that, as a result, we are poorly educated and under-skilled and our production of skilled personnel at operative, craft and technician levels, as indeed at all levels, compares unfavourably with that of our competitors. As a consequence of this belated recognition, there has been a firm commitment by the present Conservative Government, along with the other major political parties, to the improvement of our training system. The government, despite its ideological dislike of undue state involvement in the economy, has therefore between 1983 and 1987 invested four billion pounds in training, much of it on the new two-year Youth Training Scheme, and is proposing to spend a further seven billion pounds over the next four years.[46] As we have seen, among recent government initiatives, in addition to the Youth Training Scheme, are the Job Training Scheme, shortly to be reformed, for employed adults who have hitherto been largely unable to participate in MSC-funded training schemes, and the Open College which it is hoped will eventually enable millions of workers to train and retrain, mainly on an individual basis.

In addition, there is no doubt that increasing numbers of employers are becoming aware of the need to train and retrain their employees and, as a result, are prepared to invest much more readily in training programmes than has hitherto been the case. Indeed, the combination of the increasing willingness of industry and business to send their employees to be trained, and the increasing funds that have become available for this purpose — not just from the government through the MSC, but also from the European Economic Community through the European Social Fund and the European Development Fund — has led at least one authority on the subject to comment that funding training is no longer a problem, but that the supply of suitable programmes by the further education colleges has failed to keep up with recent demands.[47] Certainly, while there are many examples of successful collaboration between employers and colleges which have already resulted in excellent tailor-made provision, there still remain good resources in the colleges that are not being effectively used by employers.[48] It is partly for this reason that the private sector of further education has begun to fill the gap and take advantage of the excellent market opportunity. However, it too has reacted relatively slowly to meet the needs, and has a long way to go before it compares in extent with the private sectors in Japan and the United States, for example. None the less, the increasing recognition, both by the government and by employers, of the importance of training is a large step in the right direction; indeed, there has even been heady talk that 'the training revolution' in the United Kingdom has finally taken hold.[49]

While welcoming this belated recognition of the importance of training, a more considered reaction would be to recognise that we still have a very long way to go before our training system matches in effectiveness and comprehensiveness those of our industrial competitors. Compared to West Germany, for example, where some 600,000 young people every year enter a three-year programme leading to a nationally-recognised qualification, the United Kingdom's apprenticeship system has substantially declined over the past decade, and the Youth Training Scheme has only recently become a two-year programme with a substantial job-specific content. Moreover, our system of vocational qualifications is complex, not to say baffling, and the National Council for Vocational Qualifications has only just taken on the difficult task of producing a logical and progressive framework.

In any case, it can be convincingly argued that in order to produce a highly-skilled work force, the foundations must be laid in the school system, and that higher standards of basic education, especially of literacy and numeracy, are a prerequisite. In addition, this basic structure needs to be supplemented by a much higher participation rate in full-time education after compulsory schooling. In this latter respect we lag far behind Japan and the United States, for example, where as we have seen, the great majority of young people stay on in full-time education until age 18 and thereafter many of them enter some form of full-time post-secondary education and training. These high levels of participation depend very much upon parental encouragement and a willingness to invest heavily in their children's education, a social climate which cannot easily or rapidly be induced. In the meantime, the United Kingdom remains one of the few industrial countries in which the majority of 16-year-olds try to enter the labour market.[50]

Partly for this reason, there is considerable confusion in the United Kingdom between the roles of education and training and the further education colleges, in particular, are caught up in this dilemma. Traditionally, they have seen themselves as offering youngsters a mixed diet of education and training, a role which is highly desirable given that so many of them leave school too soon and with inadequate educational backgrounds. However, as we have seen, during recent years the environment of further education has been changing, with the colleges having more and more to adopt the training policies determined and financed by the Manpower Services Commission. The main reason for this state of affairs is the lack of resources made available for education, both in the colleges and in the school system. It is high time that there was a much wider understanding in the United Kingdom that human resources are our greatest national asset, which should be fostered with the sort of enthusiasm that the Japanese display, by the pursuit of vigorous policies and the provision of adequate resources throughout our system of education and training.[51]

If we are to make the best use of our human resources, then we must

147

make greater efforts to harness the potential of those groups in our society who are, to different degrees, disadvantaged. These include both girls and women, and also the ethnic minorities. As in all the developed countries described in this book, sexual stereotyping occurs widely in the United Kingdom, with young men being channelled into 'male' occupations and young women into 'female' ones. Although some attempts have been made to persuade girls and women to think more widely of possible careers, these have not been very successful. While more resources devoted to this end would undoubtedly help, the problem may be more a matter of changing the priorities of those who inform and advise young people of their choice of training. These include not just the staff of further education colleges, but also schools, employers, MSC staff and, above all, the careers service.[52]

The same is true of many young people in the ethnic minorities. There is evidence that the major reason why many black people, for example, do not fully avail themselves of training opportunities in the further education colleges is the existence of 'a serious information gap' between the colleges and the communities.[53] Among the latter, there is a lack of information about the nature of the futher education colleges and about what specific courses are available in particular colleges. Where colleges have designed 'Access' or other courses particularly for these groups, however, they have frequently elicited a very positive response. What is needed, therefore, is both a concerted effort to inform the ethnic minority communities more fully of what the further education colleges have to offer them and also a modification of current provision to meet their needs more effectively.

Finally, a major factor in ensuring economic success seems to be the appreciation by industry and business of the importance of training and a willingness to invest substantially in it. As we have seen, British industry lags behind that in Japan and the United States, partly because, as in Australia, it has been content to rely on the further education colleges to provide much of the training. Although there are welcome signs that parts of British industry are waking up to the critical importance of training and are, therefore, more willing to devote some of their resources to it, others are still reluctant to do so. What are needed are more incentives to do so.

Chapter six

Conclusions and Comparisons

Perhaps the most obvious and striking feature of the systems of vocational education and training of the five countries described in this book is the way in which they faithfully reflect the characteristics of the societies of which they are part. It is a truism well known to every student of comparative education that educational systems as a whole are microcosms of the societies of which they are part, a truism which applies *a fortiori* to vocational education and training. This is well illustrated, for example, by a consideration of the role of the state, that is, the central government, in the provision of vocational education and training in each of the five countries.

Perhaps the most highly centralised state is Japan where, mainly for historical and traditional reasons, the central government has largely determined the nature and content of the publicly-run educational system. The same is true of the public vocational training institutions which, however, are run not by the Japanese Ministry of Education but by the Ministry of Labour, a system which finds increasing echoes in the United Kingdom, as the role of the Department of Employment, through the Manpower Services Commission, grows larger and, recently, in Australia, with the creation of a new 'super-ministry', the Department of Education, Employment and Training. However, in Japan an essentially conservative political philosophy reigns, the private sector of vocational education and training is encouraged, and is flourishing as a result.

In the United Kingdom, by contrast, the role of the central government in our system of vocational education and training has, until quite recently, been relatively small. Instead, in keeping with the administration of the educational system in general, much of the responsibility for providing courses for training operatives, craftsmen, technicians, and the like, has been in the hands of the local education authorities through their technical colleges and colleges of further education. Industry in its turn has relied to a great extent on the maintained colleges to train its skilled personnel. In recent years, however, the government has come increasingly to believe, rightly or wrongly, that one cause of our economic and social problems is our inadequate system of vocational education and training, that, in other words, our ill-prepared work force is a prime cause of our industrial and economic decline.[1] While the causes of the United Kingdom's very poor record in training its workers are many and complex and include social, economic, industrial, and educational factors, nevertheless it is natural and, to an extent inevitable, that governments should adopt a more interventionist policy towards vocational education and training. In the United Kingdom the Manpower Services Commission has been the prime instrument of that policy. At the same time, the political beliefs of the Conservative Government have led them to stimulate, not always directly or overtly, the role of the private sector in providing vocational education and training

In the case of Australia similar trends are occurring. Here, for geographical and historical reasons, a federal structure has operated for most of the present century, with considerable power and authority being vested in the states so that, until relatively recently, the Commonwealth Government in Canberra has been content to leave the determination of vocational education and training very largely to the states themselves. However, as in the United Kingdom, the worsening of Australia's economic circumstances in recent years, and the belief of the Commonwealth Government that an essential requirement for industrial and economic growth is the training of a more highly skilled work force has led it to intervene much more substantially and directly in the country's financing and overall structure of vocational education and training. As in the United Kingdom, this process seems likely to accelerate over the next few years.

In the United States, paradoxically, the coming into office of the Reagan administration with its ideological commitment to reducing the role of the federal government and enhancing 'states' rights has, during the 1980s, led to a very large reduction in the amount of federal aid to vocational education and training across the country. In any case, as the responsibility for educational provision has been, and remains, that of each of the fifty states, and as each is free to decide on the priority it wishes to accord to the provision of vocational education and training, there are very considerable variations between one state and another. Moreover, individual states may choose to devolve educational powers on smaller administrative units, the local districts, so there are frequently considerable variations in provision within states themselves. Finally, although the role of the private sector of vocational education and training is important across the United States as a whole, it too varies considerably from one part of the very large country to another.

West Germany, too, is a federal country with considerable responsibilities for the provision of vocational education and training devolved to the eleven state governments, or *Länder*. Here, however, the Federal

Government plays an important role in an administrative structure in which each of the major partners, including employers and trades unions, have a clearly-defined part to play. For example, the general structure of vocational education and training has been specified by a number of Federal Vocational Training Acts and the 'Dual System' which has resulted is the product of a complex arrangement which relies for its success on shared responsibility, management and finance among the Federal, *Länder* and municipal governments, the employers, and the trades unions.[2]

Another important feature of the five national systems of vocational education and training described in the book is one we have already touched upon, namely, the contribution, to a greater or lesser extent, of the private sector. In this context, as elsewhere in the book, the term 'private sector' is taken to mean those private institutions, outside the maintained state sectors, which offer programmes of vocational education and training, thus excluding training provided within industry and business itself. Inevitably, as every student of comparative studies will testify, confusion arises over the use of terminology: as we have seen, in the United States, for example, the term 'private sector' is used to denote what we have here excluded, namely, training provided within industry itself. However, used in the way we have described it, the private sector's role varies enormously: in Japan and the United States, for example, it plays a major role, the United Kingdom contribution to vocational education and training is growing, while in the Federal Republic of Germany it is relatively unimportant, though this is because of the major role played by industry and commerce. These differences are to a considerable extent the product of differing political philosophies, so that in the United States and Japan, for example, where private entrepreneurship is encouraged, the private sector flourishes. Thus, Japan's Special Training and Miscellaneous Schools, and American private proprietorial vocational colleges, loom large in the national systems of vocational education and training. In the United Kingdom and Australia, by contrast, a different tradition obtains. In these countries, the private sector has been relatively small and the great bulk of vocational education and training has been provided by what are called 'maintained' colleges, that is, institutions financed very largely out of the public purse. However, as we have seen, the situation in the United Kingdom has changed somewhat in recent years as private institutions have both grown in number and expanded in size, mainly in direct response to the growth of the Youth Training Scheme and the willingness of the Manpower Services Commission to commission training programmes from them.

This growth brings into sharper focus the nature and extent of the role which the private sector could and should play in the United Kingdom training system. On the one hand, the private colleges offer obvious advantages: they can and do respond very quickly to labour market demands; they offer courses almost entirely job-specific in character, which, because they therefore contain little or no general education and do not bother much with holidays, are shorter and, by strictly utilitarian standards, more cost-efficient than comparable courses in the maintained colleges. If American experience is anything to go by, they also set out to attract students by placing before them the minimum of bureaucratic procedures, and for this reason are often favoured by students from ethnic minorities. The better colleges also claim, with some justice it would seem, to be very successful in placing their products in jobs once they have completed their courses. On the other hand, there is no doubt that for the students who patronise them their courses are very expensive compared to those offered by the publicly-run colleges; for this reason, it is much more common for students to drop in and out and for the overall wastage rate to be higher. The private colleges also operate across a relatively limited range of subjects, for the most part those in which the investment in capital equipment is not unduly high. Thus, in the United Kingdom, Japan and the United States, they tend to be most common in such areas as secretarial studies, computer studies, and beauty therapy. Moreover, there are very considerable variations in the standards of the teaching and facilities which they offer and, undoubtedly, a proportion of them are more concerned with making profits for their owners than ensuring that high standards are maintained. For this reason alone, if their numbers are to grow in the United Kingdom, as seems very likely, it is important that the Department of Education and Science and the Manpower Services Commission between them institute an effective system of inspection and registration. As things stand at present, not only does such a system not exist, but accurate figures of the numbers of private colleges currently in existence and the numbers of students they contain are not available.

Another major area in which there are considerable variations between one country and another is the attitude taken to industrial training by employers, and the contribution which they make to it. In Japan, as we have seen, among the large corporations at least, the development of the skills and indeed the allegiance to the companies of their work forces are accorded a very high priority. This is partly a recognition of the fact that in a country very lacking in basic raw materials, the abilities of its peoples constitute a major resource to be fully utilised. Hence, the government and employers have recently been placing increasing emphasis on the importance, not just of initial vocational training, but also on retraining and skill updating to which it attaches the significant appellation of 'Human Resources Development'. To these ends Japanese companies are willing to invest considerable sums of money in vocational educa- tion and training and, as we have seen, the great majority of such training is provided by industry itself. The inculcation of skills training is facilitated by the fact that, generally speaking, employers can take for granted that their new employees come to them from school, or college, with a very sound and thorough general education.

To a degree, a similar situation obtains in the United States, in that the large companies and corporations are prepared to spend very considerable sums of money on the training of their employees. In America, as virtually everywhere else, including Japan, small concerns find it much more difficult to finance and provide training facilities. However, a significant development in the course of the 1980s has been the considerable increase in the amount of training provided by most of the large American companies, ascribed in large part to technological changes which necessitate retraining and the updating of skills, and to foreign competition which has caused American industry to seek improvements in the proficiency of its employees. In the United States, like Japan, there is a very wide dissemination of education, with a substantial proportion of young people staying on at school until aged 18 and then moving into some form of vocational training. Despite the trenchant criticisms levelled at the American high school that its academic standards are too low and have fallen in the last twenty years or so, nevertheless the American desire for continuing education and the openness of the system do ensure that it reaches a much higher proportion of the population than in the United Kingdom.

In West Germany, as in Japan, the majority of industrial training is provided on-the-job, by industry itself, though the quality and length of such training varies somewhat from one occupation to another. However, the fact that training costs are largely borne by the training firms is symptomatic of a national attitude and tradition whereby employers expect, and are expected, to provide both initial industrial training and, to a lesser extent, retraining and skills updating. While this attitude could be regarded as self-serving in that employers use their control of training as a means of inculcating good work habits and of developing a highly skilled work force, nevertheless they are also conscious that it has other virtues such as creating social stability by giving their employees, especially young school-leavers, a status and a place in society.[3]

By contrast, the 'British' tradition, as exemplified by Australia and the United Kingdom, has operated in a different fashion. In Australia, the sheer vastness of the country and the wide dispersion of population around its periphery, together with the relatively small size of the domestic market, have made it difficult and expensive for all but the largest companies to provide much in the way of industrial training. In any case, until quite recently Australia has not considered it necessary to introduce firm national policies for the development of skills training. In the circumstances, it is quite natural that industry should rely very largely on the Colleges of Technical and Further Education for this purpose. As we have seen, the economic recession of the last few years and the increase in youth unemployment have caused the Commonwealth Government to take a much stronger position which includes, among other things, the stimulation of industry and business to provide much more industrial training themselves.

In the United Kingdom, a similar tradition has operated, whereby the further education colleges have provided the theoretical underpinning of skills training. The stake of industry itself in providing training has, unfortunately, been a limited one. While many of the larger well-known firms have proved training comparable in quality and effectiveness to that in West Germany, too many have provided little or no adequate training, and in general the sort of commitment to training by industry, so typical of West Germany, has been largely absent in the United Kingdom.[4] One major reason for this reluctance by many employers to invest in training is their oft-repeated complaint that money spent by individual companies is often wasted, as no sooner have they trained a skilled worker than he or she is 'poached' by a rival company which has made no such investment. Attempts at improving this situation by legislation, such as the Industrial Training Act of 1964 and the consequent creation of Industrial Training Boards, have proved less than successful. What is required is a substantial change in attitude by industry which recognises that investment in training contributes both to the success of industry as a whole and also to the well-being of the individual and to the strengthening of the fabric of society. As we have seen, during the last few years there are welcome signs that employers' attitudes are changing for the better, though whether they go as far as constituting 'a training revolution', as some have claimed, is open to question.

One of the major themes touched upon in the book has been the role of women and girls in vocational education and training. As we have seen, in most, if not all, of the countries examined, the contribution of women to the economy, as measured by their participation in the work force, has grown steadily over the pasty twenty years or so. However, although there has been some overall improvement in their condition relative to that of men, they still remain disadvantaged. In virtually every country, they are restricted or restrict themselves to a limited number of occupations, such as secretarial work, nursing and primary school teaching, while in Japan, with its highly successful economy, they scarcely feature in the upper echelons of industry and business, and as yet little has been done in practice to accord them greater opportunity. In Japan, as in the United States, the United Kingdom and West Germany, vocational training for women more often than not leads to employment which is characterised by lower pay than for men, less security of tenure, less opportunity for promotion, and considerable physical and psychological demands. Some countries have introduced measures to improve the situation, such as the legislation promoting 'sex-equity' in the United States and the 'alternative action' programmes introduced by TAFE colleges in Australia. However, such measures are of themselves unlikely to change matters greatly, while the deeply-ingrained attitudes of society, and indeed of women themselves, remain unaffected. A much more effective catalyst of action, in those countries subject to it, is the decline in the size of the age groups entering the working force over the next decade or so. In Japan, the United States and the United Kingdom, for example, this phenomenon will surely require industry and business, and government, to train girls and women over a much wider range of skills than is presently the case?

The same is also true for young people from ethnic minorities, whose skills are likely to be in greater demand in the foreseeable future. Like girls and women, they are presently substantially disadvantaged. Whether they are members of what in the United Kingdom are officially described as 'people of New Commonwealth and Pakistani origin', blacks and Hispanics in the United States, South-East Asian immigrants and Aboriginals in Australia, Koreans and untouchables in Japan, or Turkish and southern European *gastarbeiter* in West Germany, they suffer disproportionately from unemployment. For a whole variety of social and economic reasons, too many of them do not achieve the qualifications which their ability and potential would suggest, and leave school hostile to formal education which many of them see as irrelevant to their needs. Partly for this reason, their take up of vocational education and training is unnecessarily limited. As with women, attempts have been made to help them in some of the countries described in this book by, for example, the provision of special 'access' courses, made up of specifically designed programmes to develop skills similar to those provided by more traditional courses but more suited to their experience and future needs. Where appropriate — as in Australia, the United States and the United Kingdom — their special curriculum needs are, to some extent, catered for by the provision of courses designed to enable them to acquire a good standard of written and spoken English. Inevitably, many unemployed youngsters from ethnic minorities find their way into the new training programmes such as the Youth Training Scheme in the United Kingdom, the Job Training Partnership Act in the United States, and the Australian Traineeship System. How far these programmes will enable them to acquire the skills which they need to obtain and hold down good jobs in industry and business remains to be seen.

Another vitally important aspect of vocational education and training described and analysed in the book is the training and development of teachers and instructors of vocational subjects. In this regard, too, practice varies widely from country to country. Perhaps the most systematic arrangements are those in Australia where in all the states, with the sole exception of South Australia, teachers in TAFE colleges are required to undertake a course of professional training. In the United Kingdom, with the exception of Northern Ireland, no such requirement is enforced, though slightly more than half the teachers in colleges of further education and technical colleges have voluntarily undertaken such a course. In the United States, the situation is a much more complex and confusing one, with considerable differences in requirements from one state to another: here, especially in the high schools, there is a serious shortage of teachers of vocational education, similar to that of teachers of craft, design and technology in British schools. For this reason, in some states the requirement for them to have successfully completed a course of teacher education is no longer mandatory.

In the United Kingdom some progress has been made in the provision both of initial training courses for teachers and instructors in colleges and in industry, and also of staff development programmes for those with experience. In the former respect, the development in the past decade of a regional network of part-time, in-service initial training courses for further education teachers leading to CNAA Certificates and the expansion of City and Guilds 730 courses is significant. So, too, is the network of Accredited Training Centres established by the Manpower Services Commission to provide training programmes for both workplace supervisors and further education staff. As far as staff development programmes are concerned, these, too, have increased in number, whether offered by some of the further education colleges, by the Further Education Staff College, by the Manpower Services Commission, or by industry itself. Overall, however, provision is patchy and among the most pressing needs for both teachers and instructors are recent industrial experience and skills updating, made all the more urgent by rapid technological changes.

However, the United Kingdom still has a very long way to go before there is sufficient and systematic provision on a national basis, and this will only occur if substantially more money is invested in training and staff development by government and industry. This investment will need to take various forms in order to meet the multiplicity of needs and of regional and local circumstances, but one initiative worth considering might well be the establishment of a national Institute of Vocational Training, along the lines of the one which flourishes in Japan. Like its Japanese counterpart, it might be charged with the responsibility of training teachers and instructors for both further education colleges and industrial training centres. Certainly, whether or not such an institution is established, the training needs of both further education teachers and workplace trainers will have to be properly met and co-ordinated if the standards of British vocational education training are to be significantly raised. It is one of the encouraging features of the establishment of the National Council for Vocational Qualifications, whose remit includes the rationalisation of the educational and training elements of vocational qualifications, that it has begun to stimulate an awareness of the need to develop a national strategy for staff development for both further education teachers and also workplace trainers, and to bring the two groups closer together.

It is quite clear that throughout the developed world rapid changes in technology are causing governments to conclude that the quantity and quality of skills training of the work force must be increased. How best to achieve this end is, of course, another matter. In the United Kingdom the government has assumed that what is needed is 'a new vocationalism', including the introduction of a national training system for school-leavers, of which the Youth Training Scheme is a major part, and the moving of the secondary school curriculum in a vocational direction by means of such curricular developments as the Technical and Vocational Education Initiative and the Certificate of Pre-Vocational Education. Significantly, this drive to introduce more vocationalism into the secondary schools and tertiary sector in the United Kingdom is spearheaded, not by the Department of Education and Science, but by the Manpower Services Commission. However, it is by no means certain that this is the best way of providing more and more highly skilled young people; indeed, another model is the Japanese one, where young people receive a sound general education, more or less universally up to age of 18, upon which an effective system of training, very largely industry-based, can be erected. Certainly, many British employers believe that, especially in an age of rapidly changing technology, schools would do better to concentrate on imparting general education. However, to achieve the Japanese or even American, levels of participation in full-time education, after the statutory school-leaving age, would require such fundamental changes of attitude in British society as to be very unlikely of achievement in anything but the long term. Perhaps, therefore, the long-established and effective West German *Dual System*, with its mixture of vocational training and general education, provides a more practicable model to emulate. Whichever way the United Kingdom chooses to go, whether by design or accident, a concentration on narrow vocational training at the expense of general education for young people, or 'human resource development' for adults, is unlikely to achieve success. In an increasingly complex world affected by an exponential rate of technological innovation, the need to develop creative thinking and an ability to innovate among our work force has never been greater. Therefore, a successful system of vocational education and training in the United Kingdom is likely to be one which recognises and promotes a 'dual mandate', [5] namely the education and vocational training of the individual both in his own interest and for that of the economy. The United Kingdom has a long way to go, however, before it has such a system in place.

Notes and References

Introduction

1. John Twining *et al.* (eds) (1987) *Vocational Education*, World Yearbook of Education 1987, Kogan Page, p. 11.
2. This definition follows that adopted in Christopher Hayes *et al.*, (1984) *Competence and Competition*, University of Sussex Institute of Manpower Studies, p. 2.
3. Twining op. cit., p. 12.

1 Japan: a well-ordered society

1. Leonard Cantor (1985) 'Vocational Education and Training: the Japanese approach', *Comparative Education*, 21(1): 67–76.
2. Christopher Hayes *et al.*, (1984) *Competence and Competition*, University of Sussex Institute of Manpower Studies.
3. DES/Society of Education Officers (1986) 'Joint Report on a Visit to Japan'.
4. Robert C. Christopher (1984) *The Japanese Mind: the Goliath explained*, Pan; Benjamin Duke (1986) *The Japanese School, Lessons for Industrial America*, Praeger; and T.P. Rohlen (1983) *Japan's High Schools*, University of California Press. In addition a very informative and up-to-date summary of the Japanese educational system is to be found in *Japanese Education Today*, US Department of Education, 1987.
5. Hayes, op. cit., p. 52.
6. Robert R. Rehder (1983) 'Education and Training: have the Japanese beaten us again?' *Personnel Journal* (USA), 62(1): 42.
7. Benjamin Duke, op cit.
8. Amano Ikuo (1986) 'The Dilemma of Japanese Education Today', *Japan Foundation Newsletter*, XIII (5 March): 8.
9. S.J. Prais (1987) 'Education for Productivity: comparisons of Japanese and English Schooling and vocational preparation', *Compare*, 16(2): 121–47.
10. See, for example, National Council on Educational Reform (1987) *Fourth and Final Report on Educational Reform*.

11. National Institute for Educational Research (1986) *Basic Facts and Figures About the Educational System in Japan*, Tokyo, p. 8.
12. S.J. Prais, op. cit., p. 136.
13. Association of National Technical Colleges (1982) *The Technical Colleges in Japan*, Tokyo, p. 2.
14. For a fuller account, see Leonard Cantor (1987) 'The Role of the Private Sector in Vocational Education and Training: The Case of Japan's Special Training Schools', *The Vocational Aspect of Education*, XXXIX(103): 35–41.
15. Toshio Ishikawa (1987) *Vocational Training*, The Japanese Institute of Labour, revised edn, p. 7.
16. W.G. McDerment (1984/5) *New Technologies, Education and Vocational Training in Japan*, Berlin: European Centre for the Development of Vocational Training (CEDEFOP), p. 21.
17. Toshio Ishikawa, op. cit., p. 30.
18. DES/SEO Report, op. cit., p. 14.
19. Leonard Cantor (1984) 'The Institute of Vocational Training, Japan', *BACIE Journal*, 39(6): 211–13.
20. Toshio Ishikawa, op. cit., pp. 21–9.
21. G.W. Ford (1986) 'Learning from Japan: The Concept of Skill Formation', *Australian Bulletin of Labour*, 12(2): p. 123.
22. Gene Gregory (1986) *Japanese Electronics Technology: Enterprise and Innovation*, John Wiley, pp. 124–5.
23. Bill Ford 'A learning society: Japan through Australian eyes', chapter 20 in John Twining, *et al.* (eds) (1987) *Vocational Education*, World Yearbook of Education 1987, Kogan Page, pp. 264–76.
24. Christopher Hayes, op. cit., p. 44.
25. DES/SEO Report, op. cit., p. 7.

2   Australia: the tyranny of distance

1. *The Commonwealth Government's Strategy for Young People*, Canberra: Office of Youth Affairs 1987, p. 6.
2. Peter Karmel (1985) 'Trends and Issues in Australian Education, 1970–1985', *Report of International Seminar on Educational Reform*, October, Kyoto University, Japan, p. 1.
3. The Commonwealth Government announced at the end of 1987 that the CTEC will be abolished and will be replaced by a statutory board of employment, education, and training, made up of representatives of business, industry, the trades unions, and education. It will report directly to the Minister for Employment, Education and Training and will have four advisory councils — on higher education, research, the school sector, and employment and skills formation — which will report publicly on its advice to the Minister, as does the CTEC at present. One major effect of the changes will be a shift in authority towards the Commonwealth Department of Education, Employment and Training.
4. *New South Wales TAFE Handbook*, vol. 1: Administration, Sydney:

New South Wales Department of TAFE, 1986, p. 25.

5. *TAFE in Australia* (Kangan report), Canberra: Report of the Australian Committee of Technical and Further Education, 1974.

6. *TAFE Triennial Planning Submission, 1985–1987*, vol. 1, Sydney: New South Wales Department of Technical and Further Education, 1983, p. 13.

7. Ray Grannall (1985) *Regionalisation for TAFE: An Evaluation of the System of Regionalisation in New South Wales*, Sydney: New South Wales Department of TAFE, p. 3.

8. Norman T. Pyle (1986) 'Principalship in Colleges offering NAFE in the North-West of England and Further Education in Queensland', unpublished University of Lancaster PhD, p. 25.

9. John Ainley and Jeff Clancy (1983) 'Entry to the Skilled Trades in Australia: the role of family background and school achievement', *Research in Science and Technological Education*, 1(2): 145.

10. 'Submission to the Review of TAFE Funding', Canberra: Department of Employment and Industrial Relations, Canberra: 1986, p. 33.

11. *Skills for Australia*, Canberra: Australian Government Publishing Service, 1987, p. 57.

12. 'The Implementation of a Youth Employment Program', *Australian Journal of Public Administration*, 46(1) (March 1987): 66–76.

13. Norman T. Pyle (1986) 'TAFE: Productivity and Equity', *Australian Journal of TAFE Research and Development*, 2(1): 73–4.

14. Kathleen Mackie (1985) 'The Australian Traineeship System: Issues and Strategies', paper presented to National TAFE Conference, November; Mackie (1986) 'Traineeships: A New System of Vocational Training', *Australian Journal of TAFE Research and Development*, 2(1): 34–47.

15. Nicholas Clark and Associates (1987) *An Evaluation of Standards-Based Trade Training*, National Training Council, January, p. 56.

16. *Skills for Australia*, op. cit., p. 72.

17. This section of the chapter draws heavily on Gerald Burke and Denis Davis (1986) 'Ethnic Groups and Post-compulsory Education', in *Migrants, Labour Markets and Training programs, Studies of the Migrant Youth Work Force*, Melbourne: Australian Institute of Multicultural Affairs.

18. *Reducing the Risk, Report on Unemployed Youth and Labour Market Programmes*, Melbourne: Australian Institute of Multicultural Affairs, March 1985.

19. *TAFE Triennial Planning Submission, 1985–1987*, op. cit., p. 20.

20. G.W. Ford (1984) 'Australia at Risk: An Underskilled and Vulnerable Society', in Jill Eastwood et al. (eds) *Labour Essays, 1984*, Melbourne, p. 61.

21. Ibid., p. 62.

22. Queensland Department of TAFE (1985) *Future Provision, TAFE Distance Education*, February, p. 2.

23. Richard Lancaster et al. (1986) 'Non-Starters in a TAFE External Studies Institution', *Australian Journal of TAFE Research and*

Development, 2(1): 94–5.

24. *Future Provision, TAFE Distance Education*, op. cit., p. 7.
25. David Beswick (1987) 'Trends in Australian Higher Education Research: a general view', *Studies in Higher Education*, 12(2) 47.
26. Hugh Hudson (1984) 'Participation and Equity in Tertiary Education', *Proceedings, National Conference on the Participation and Equity Program*, Canberra, September, p. 23.
27. For a description of the content and organisation of a similar programme in South Australia, see R. Sumner (1983) 'The Preparation of Further Educators in South Australia', *British Journal of In-Service Education*, 9(2): 115–19.
28. A. Fordham and J. Ainley (1980) *The Evaluation of Staff Development in Technical and Further Education*, Melbourne: Australian Council for Educational Research.
29. William Hall (1986) 'An Investigation into the Pre-Service and In-Service Education of Full-time TAFE Teachers and Principals', TAFE National Centre for Research and Development, p. 18.
30. Maurice Hayes (1986) 'A Process Model for Skill Formation — An Industry Point of View', *Australian Journal of TAFE Research and Development*, 2(1): 17.
31. Trevor Prescott (1986) 'The TAFE/Industry Interface', *Australian Journal of TAFE Research and Development* 2(1): 9.
32. *The Review of Youth Policies in Australia*, Draft Report, Paris: Organization for Economic co-operation and Development, November 1984, para. 95.
33. Bill Ford (1987) 'A Learning Society: Japan through Australian eyes', in John Twining et al. (eds), *Vocational Education*, World Yearbook of Education 1987, Kogan Page, p. 270.
34. *Skills for Australia*, op. cit., p. 34.
35. Len Cantor and Peter West (1986) 'Staff Development: The Way Ahead for TAFE', *Australian Journal of TAFE Research and Development*, 2(1): 101.
36. Richard Sweet (1984) 'Australian Trends in Job Skill Requirements', revised version of paper presented to US-Australia Joint Seminar on the Future Impact of Technology on Work and Education, Monash University, Clayton, Victoria, September, p. 26.

3 The United States of America: a unique diversity

1. For example, a short, informative, and very useful introduction to the American scene and its educational system, together with a bibliography, can be found in Edmund King (1979) *Other Schools and Ours*, Holt, Rinehart and Winston, 5th edn, chapter 8.
2. Chester E. Finn, Jr (1985) 'Education Reform in the United States: Trends and Issues Introduction', Paper presented to an International Seminar on Educational Reform, Chiba and Kyoto, Japan, October, p. 1.
3. Leonard M. Cantor (1980) 'The Growing Role of the States in American Education', *Comparative Education*, 16(1): 25–31.

4. John Hillison and William G. Camp (1985) 'History and Future of the Dual School System for Vocational Education', *Journal of Vocational and Technical Education*, 2(1): 48–56, Omicron Tau Theta.

5. The National Commission on Secondary Vocational Education (n.d.) *The Unfinished Agenda: The Role of Vocational Education in the High Schools*, Columbus, Ohio: The National Center for Research in Vocational Education, p. 2.

6. Ibid., p. 11.

7. David Stern et al., (1986) *One Million Hours A Day: Vocational Education in California Public Schools, Policy Analysis for California Education (PACE)*, University of California, Berkeley, Cal.: School of Education, March.

8. T. Lewis and M.V. Lewis (1985) 'Vocational Education in the Commonwealth Caribbean and the United States', *Comparative Education*, 12(2): 166.

9. See, for example, *Design Papers for the National Assessment of Vocational Education*, Washington, DC: US Department of Education, 1987; and Proceedings of a Symposium on 'Re-Visioning Vocational Education in the Secondary School', 1987 Annual Meeting of the American Educational Research Association, Washington, DC.

10. Stern, *et al.*, op. cit., p. 21.

11. C.J. Hurn (1983) 'The Vocationalisation of American Education', *European Journal of Education*, 18(1): 55.

12. John M. Plowman (1986) 'A Comparison of Tertiary Colleges in Britain and Community Colleges in the United States', *Journal of Further and Higher Education*, 10(1): 42–51.

13. California Post-Secondary Education Commission (1986) *Background for Expanding Educational Equity*, Sacramento, March, p. 13.

14. Commission for the Review of the Master Plan for Higher Education in California (1986) *The Challenge of Change: A Reassessment of the California Community Colleges*, Sacramento, March p. 5.

15. Ibid., pp. 9–10.

16. Graham Peeke (1986) 'Improving Further Education in Britain and America', *Journal of Further and Higher Education*, 10(3): 29–35.

17. Commission for the Review of the Master Plan for Higher Education (1986) 'What Postsecondary Education Offers in California: The Enormity of the Enterprise', Background Paper no. 4, Sacramento, July, p. 6.

18. C.J. Hurn, op. cit., p. 56.

19. Christopher Davis (1983) 'Private Trade and Technical Schools', *Vocational Education Journal*, 58(1): 28–9.

20. Christopher Hayes et al., (1984) *Competence and Competition*, University of Sussex Institute of Manpower Studies, pp. 91–2.

21. Stephen F. Hamilton and John F. Claus (1985) 'Youth Unemployment in the United States: Problems and Programmes', in Rob Fiddy (ed.) *Youth Unemployment and Training. A Collection of National Perspectives*, Falmer Press, pp. 155–6.

22. Cheryl Long (1985) 'Tapping into JTPA', *Vocational Education*

Journal, 60(3): 38–110; and Terry W. Hartle and Stuart Rosenfeld (1984) 'Beyond the Vocational Education Acts: the Federal presence in vocational education', *Vocational Education Journal*, 59(1): 24–6.

23. Paul E. Peterson and Barry G. Rabe (1987) 'Coordination of Vocational Education and Manpower Training Programs', *Design Papers for the National Assessment of Vocational Education*, op. cit., pp. iv-38.

24. Anthony Patrick Casnevale (1986) 'The Learning Enterprise', *Training and Development Journal*, 40(1): 18.

25. *Education in Industry*, The Conference Board, New York, 1977.

26. See, for example, Seymour Lusterman (1955) *Trends in Corporate Education and Training*, The Conference Board, New York; 'Employee Training in America', *Training and Development Journal*, 40(7): 34–7, July 1986; 'Training Magazine's Industry Report 1986', *Training*, 23(10), October 1986; *Serving the New Corporation*, American Society for Training and Development, 1986; and 'Training in the Private Sector', the April 1987, 62(3) edn of *Vocational Education Journal*, which is wholly devoted to the subject.

27. Nell P. Enrich (1985) *Corporate Classrooms*, Carnegie Foundation for the Advancement of Teaching.

28. *Serving the New Corporation*, op. cit., p. 3.

29. *Women Apprentices in Hawaii*, State Board for Vocational Education, University of Hawaii, August 1984, p. 3.

30. Rebecca S. Douglas (1987) 'Access to Quality Vocational Education: A Sex Equity Perspective', *Design Papers for the National Assessment of Vocational Education*, op. cit., ii-36.

31. *The Unfinished Agenda: the Role of Vocational Education in the High Schools*, op. cit., p. 15.

32. Nevin R. Frantz, Jr. (1984) 'Teaching Teachers: A Search for Quality', *Vocational Education Journal*, 59(6): 47.

33. Richard C. Erickson (1985) 'Challenges to Vocational Teacher Education', *Vocational Education Journal* 60(6): 28.

34. Gene Bottoms (1985) 'How are we Responding to Change?', *Vocational Education Journal*, 60(4):10.

35. W. Norton Grubb (1987) 'Blinding faith in the new orthodoxy', *Times Higher Education Supplement*, 26 June, p. 14.

36. Ibid.

37. Daniel B. Dunham (1986) 'An Open Letter to the Secretary of Education', *Vocational Education Journal*, 61(3):11.

4 The federal republic of Germany: a commitment to vocational education and training

1. S.J. Prais (1985) 'What Can We Learn from the German System of Education and Vocational Training?', in G.D.N. Worswick (ed.) *Education and Economic Performance*, Gower, chapter 5, p. 40.

2. Christopher Hayes *et al.* (1984) *Competence and Competition*,

University of Sussex Institute of Manpower Studies, p. 5.
3. European Centre for the Development of Vocational Training(CEDEFOP) (1987) *The role of the social partners in vocational and further training in the Federal Republic of Germany,* Berlin, p. 2.
4. Wolfgang Mitter (1985) 'Educational Reforms in the Federal Republic of Germany', Paper presented to an International Seminar on Educational Reform, Chiba and Kyoto, Japan, October, p. 6.
5. Sterling Fishman and Lothar Martin (1987) *Estranged Twins, Education and Society in the Two Germanys,* Praeger, p. 111.
6. Ibid., p. 120.
7. Paul Bendelow (1987) 'Undecided over ultimate Abitur', *Times Educational Supplement,* 13 March.
8. S.J. Prais and K. Wagner (1986) 'Schooling Standards in England and Germany: some summary comparisons bearing on economic performance', *Compare,* 16(1):22.
9. U.J. Kledzik (1985) 'Education For Below Average Pupils: Arbeitslehre — A New Field in Lower Secondary Education in Berlin', in Policy Studies Institute/Anglo-German Foundation (1985) *Thinkers and Makers, Education for Tomorrow's Society,* chapter 12, p. 88.
10. S.J. Prais and K. Wagner, op. cit.; M. Murray and J. Heywood (1986) 'Education for Work in the Federal Republic of Germany', in J. Heywood and P. Matthews, *Technology, Society and the School Curriculum: Practice and Theory in Europe,* Roundthorne, p. 103; and J. Woppel (1982) 'Arbeitslehre in the Federal Republic of Germany', in Russ Russell (ed.) *Learning About the World of Work in the Federal Republic of Germany,* Studies in Vocational Education and Training in the Federal Republic of Germany, no. 7, Further Education Staff College, 9, p. 11.
11. 'Learning for the Working World: Vocational Training in the Federal Republic of Germany', *Bildung und Wissenschaft,* 1986, Bonn, p. 13.
12. For a full, up-to-date, and very informative account of the *Dual System,* upon which this chapter draws heavily, see Frank Braun (1987) 'Vocational Training as a Link between the Schools and the Labour Market: the dual system in the Federal Republic of Germany', *Comparative Education,* 23(2):123–43.
13. DES (1986) *Education in the Federal Republic of Germany, Aspects of curriculum and assessment,* HMSO, p. 10.
14. Russ Russell *et al.* (1986) *Vocational Qualifications in Five Countries,* Coombe Lodge Report, Further Education Staff College, 19(5): 292.
15. Max Planck Institute for Human Development and Education (1983) *Between Elite and Mass Education: Education in the Federal Republic of Germany,* State University of New York Press, p. 243.
16. K. Schober (1984) 'The Education System, Vocational and Youth Unemployment in West Germany', *Compare,* 14(2):134; and Volker Koditz (1985) 'The German Federal Republic: How the State Copes with the Crisis — a Guide through the Tangle of Schemes', in Rob

Fiddy (ed.) *Youth Unemployment and Training. A Collection of National Perspectives*, Falmer Press, p. 88.

17. David Parkes and Gisela Shaw (1983) 'Britons take a Meister class', *Times Higher Education Supplement*, 5 August.
18. Frank Braun, op. cit., p. 126.
19. Max Planck Institute, op. cit., p. 249.
20. K. Schober, op. cit., p. 134.
21. 'Learning for the working world: Vocational Training in the Federal Republic of Germany', op. cit., p. 34.
22. K. Schober, op. cit., pp. 137, 141.
23. Dorothee Engelhard and Kurt Krenser (1987) 'Pressures on vocational training in the Federal Republic of Germany, in John Twining (ed.) *Vocational Education*, World Yearbook of Education 1987, Kogan Page, chapter 5, pp. 62–3.
24. CEDEFOP, op. cit., p. 47.
25. 'Learning for the working world: Vocational Training in the Federal Republic of Germany', op. cit., p. 39.
26. Max Planck Institute, op. cit., p. 212.
27. CEDEFOP, op. cit., p. 102.
28. Press and Information Office of the Federal Government (1987) *Vocational Training*, Public Document 28.
29. Joachim Schaefer (1985) 'The Second Chance — Further Vocational Training', in Policy Studies Institute/Anglo German Foundation (1985) *Thinkers and Makers, Education for Tomorrow's Society*, p. 123.
30. 'Learning for the working world: Vocational Training in the Federal Republic of Germany' op. cit., p. 21.
31. Frank Braun, op. cit., p. 124.
32. Prais and Wagner, op. cit., p. 5.
33. 'Learning for the working world: Vocational Training in the Federal Republic of Germany', op. cit., p. 3.

5 The United Kingdom: a reluctant revolution?

1. J.R. Hough (1987) *Education and the National Economy*, Croom Helm, p. 1. (the first part of the chapter draws upon this very useful book).
2. Jim Tomlinson (1986) 'Retreat from responsibility', *Times Higher Education Supplement* , 14 November, p. 13.
3. Ann E.M. Lewis (1985) *Vocational Training Systems: The United Kingdom*, European Centre for the Development of Vocational Training, 3rd edn, Berlin, p. 7.
4. See, for example, *The Educational System of England and Wales*, DES, various editions. For a succinct summary of education in the United Kingdom, see chapter 7 in Edmund J. King (1979) *Other Schools and Ours*, 5th edn, Holt Rinehart & Winston.
5. For a detailed examination of the further education sector in England and Wales, see Leonard Cantor and I.F. Roberts (1986) *Further Education Today, A Critical Review*, Routledge & Kegan Paul, 3rd fully revised edn.

6. Corelli Barnett (1986) *The Audit of War*, Macmillan.
7. This section draws upon four main sources: Cantor and Roberts; op. cit., Lewis, op. cit.; Russ Russell (1985) *Further Education and Industrial Training in England and Wales*, Further Education Staff College, revised edn; and *NAFE in Practice: An HMI Survey*, HMSO, 1987.
8. Leonard Cantor (1988) 'Further Education Colleges', in Noel Entwistle (ed.) *Handbook of Educational Ideas and Practices*, Croom Helm.
9. Towards the end of 1987, to reflect its concern with training, the government announced its intention of renaming the MSC *The Training Commission*.
10. P.G. Chapman and M.J. Tooze (1987) 'Some Economic Implications of the Youth Training Scheme', *Royal Bank of Scotland Review*, 155:17.
11. B.M. Deakin and C.F. Pratten (1987) 'Economic Effects of YTS', *Employment Gazette*, October, pp. 491–7.
12. There is a very extensive and growing literature on the Youth Training Scheme and some of the more useful books and articles on the subject include Paul G. Chapman and Michael J. Tooze (1987) *The Youth Training Scheme in the United Kingdom*, Gower; Robert Fiddy (ed.) (1985) *Youth Unemployment and Training, A Collection of National Perspectives*, Falmer Press; Stewart Ranson *et al.* (1986) *The Revolution in Education and Training*, Longman; David Raffe (1987) 'The Context of the Youth Training Scheme: an analysis of its strategy and development', *British Journal of Education and Work*, 1(1):1–31; and Brian Walker (1987) ' "Quality" and the Youth Training Scheme: the gap between rhetoric and reality in the £1 billion programme', *Journal of Further and Higher Education*, 11(1): 68–73.
13. Michael Eraut and John Burke (1986) *Improving the Quality of YTS*, University of Sussex.
14. Cynthia Cockburn (1987) *Two-Track Training: Sex Inequalities and the Youth Training Scheme*, Macmillan.
15. Raffe, op. cit., p. 5.
16. John Twining (1987) 'Updating and retraining initiatives in the UK', in John Twining (ed.) *Vocational Education*, World Yearbook of Education 1987, Kogan Page, pp. 174–86.
17. Ibid., p. 180.
18. Tony Uden (1987) 'The REPLAN Experience: a view from the centre', *Adult Education*, 60:14.
19. *NAFE in practice; An HMI Survey*, op. cit., p. 4.
20. Elizabeth Hall (1985) 'One Further Education Division's Response to the Challenge of MSC', *Journal of Further and Higher Education*, 9(1):66.
21. M. Alsop (1986) 'Non-advanced further education', *Physics Education*, 21:329.
22. John Miller, *et al.*, (1986) *Preparing for Change, the Management of Curriculum-led Institutional Development*, Further Education Unit, p. vi.
23. Michael Locke and John Bloomfield (1982) *Mapping and Reviewing*

the Pattern of 16–19 Education, Schools Council pamphlet 20, p. 9.

24. Leonard Cantor (1985) 'A Coherent Approach to the Education and Training of the 16–19 Age Group', in G.D.N. Worswick (ed.) *Education and Economic Performance*, Gower, pp. 13–24.

25. Christine Ward (1987) 'Qualifications and assessment of vocational education and training in the UK', in Twining (ed.) op. cit., pp. 247–63.

26. John McAleer (1987) 'The Introduction of Mandatory Teacher-Training in Further Education in Northern Ireland', *British Journal of Inservice Education*, 13(3):123–7.

27. 'The Way Ahead in FE Staff Development', Invitation seminar, 11–12 December 1986, Blagdon: DES/Further Education Staff College, 1987.

28. See, for example, Ernest Theodosin (1986) *Management restructuring in an FE College*, Blagdon: Further Education Staff College, and Russ Russell (1986) *Vocational Qualifications in Five Countries*, Coombe Lodge Report, 19(4), Blagdon: Further Education Staff College.

29. MSC (1987) 'Developing Trainers: MSC support for training of trainers and staff development', January.

30. Gareth Williams and Maureen Woodhall (1979) *Independent Further Education*, Policy Studies Institute, June.

31. MSC (1987) *The Funding of Vocational Education and Training*, A Consultation Document, November 1987, p. 25.

32. David Wilson (1986) 'Independent Further Education in the United Kingdom', in Len Shaw (ed.), *The Gabbitas-Thring Guide to Independent Further Education, 1986–87*, Gabbitas-Thring Publishing, p. 11.

33. Walker, op. cit., p. 71; and 'The Great Training Robbery: an Interim report on the role of private training agencies within the Youth Training Scheme in the Birmingham and Solihull area', NATFHE Birmingham Liaison Committee, January 1984.

34. Elizabeth Hall, op. cit., p. 70.

35. MSC, *The Funding of Vocational Education and Training*, op. cit., p. 25.

36. Howard Davies and Martin Rispin (1987) 'The Role of Academia in Providing Training for Industry', *Journal of Further and Higher Education*, 11(1):46–8.

37. Peter Ashworth, *et al*, (1987) 'Report of the working party on demand as perceived by those who have passed through a course of management education at either undergraduate or postgraduate level', Sheffield Polytechnic.

38. Further Education Unit (1985) *Vocational Education and Training in Distribution*, December, Blagdon; and (1986) *Youth Training in the Distributive Trades*, National Economic Development Office Books.

39. Cited in 'Technicians for Prosperity', NAB/UGC Continuing Education Standing Committee, December 1986, p. 2.

40. D. Storey and S. Johnson (1987) *Job Generation and Labour Market Change*, Macmillan.

41. Peter Bill (1987) 'Deeply Flawed', *Guardian*, 21 August, p. 20.

42. Further Education Unit (1987) *Information Technology, who needs it? : an industry/college interaction*, Blagdon.
43. Summary of address by Shirley Williams reported in *EDUCA*, no. 74, June 1987, p. 10.
44. Helen Connor and Alan Gordon (1985) 'Provision for technician training', *Times Higher Education Supplement*, 22 March, p. viii.
45. Christopher Huhne (1987) 'Is industry aware there is a skills gap?', *The Guardian*, 29 April, citing an April 1987 report by Charles Handy of the London Business School, on British managers, published by the National Economic Development Office.
46. Robert Taylor (1987) 'The Thick Man of Europe', *The Observer*, 12 April, p. 24.
47. Eric Willis (1987) 'Sight of Victory', *Times Higher Education Supplement*, 30 January, p. 15.
48. Institute of Personnel Management (1986) *A Partnership in Learning*, DES, September.
49. Edward Fennell (1987) 'The Training Revolution: A Special Report', *The Times*, 6 April, p. 14.
50. Tom Johnston (1987) 'Manpower Policy — Pragmatism or Principles?', *Royal Bank of Scotland Review*, 155:10.
51. Ibid., p. 13.
52. Tessa Blackstone (1987) 'Review of Cynthia Cockburn', *Times Higher Education Supplement*, 25 September, p. 21.
53. Further Education Unit (1985) *Black Perspectives on FE Provision*, Blagdon, p. 2.

6 Conclusions and comparisons

1. Ruth Jonathan (1986) 'Vocational guidance' — a review of recent books on vocational education and training in the *Times Higher Education Supplement*, 5 December.
2. Frank Braun (1987) 'Vocational Training as a Link between the Schools and the Labour Market: the dual system in the Federal Republic of Germany', *Comparative Education*, 23(2):123–43.
3. Christopher Hayes *et al.* (1984) *Competence and Competition*, University of Sussex, Institute of Manpower Studies, p. 13.
4. M. Murray and J. Heywood (1986) 'Education for Work in the Federal Republic of Germany', in J. Heywood and P. Matthews (eds) *Technology, Society and the School Curriculum: Practice and Theory in Europe*, Roundthorne Publishing, p. 105.
5. John Twining (ed.) (1987) *Vocational Education*, World Yearbook of Education 1987, Kogan Page, p. 12.

Index